MARIA SCOTT has worked as an ~~~~~~~~~~
newspapers, specializing in persona~~~~~~~~~~
variety of other publications on busi~~~~~~~~~~
was born and educated in New Ze~~~~~ ~~~ ~~~~~~ as a journalist there
before moving to the UK. She is now based in New Zealand again and
continues to write about finance and related topics for British and New
Zealand publications.

The Daily Telegraph

How to Avoid the
INHERITANCE
TAX TRAP

Revised edition for 2007–8

Maria Scott

ROBINSON
London

Constable & Robinson Ltd
3 The Lanchesters
162 Fulham Palace Road
London W6 9ER
www.constablerobinson.com

First published in the UK by Robinson,
an imprint of Constable & Robinson Ltd 2006

This new edition published in the UK by Robinson,
an imprint of Constable & Robinson Ltd 2007

A copy of the British Library Cataloguing in
Publication Data is available from the British Library

ISBN: 978-1-84529-002-3

Printed and bound in the EU

1 3 5 7 9 10 8 6 4 2

For Paul, who really has come a long way with me

Contents

Acknowledgements

I wish to thank the following individuals and firms of professional advisers who so willingly shared their knowledge, expertise and time.

My friend and former colleague Neasa MacErlean; Jacqueline Thomson, Smith & Williamson, accountants; Gillian Cardy, Professional Partnerships, independent financial adviser (IFA); John Whiting, Valerie Smart, Simon Tees and international colleagues at PricewaterhouseCoopers, accountants; Alison Paul, Turcan Connell, solicitors; Anne Lewis and Mary-Anne Gribbon, Cripps Harries Hall, solicitors; Toby Harris, Toby Harris Tax Consultancy; Dawn Alderson, Russell-Cooke, solicitors; Nathalie Trousset-Fawcett, De Pinna, notaries; Jonathan Miller, Windram Miller, solicitors; Withers, solicitors; Matthew Pitcher, Towry Law (IFA); Iain Tyrer and Patrick O'Leary, Skipton Financial Services, financial advisers; Mike Warburton and Ian Miles, Grant Thornton, accountants; Kevin Carr, Lifesearch, life insurance broker and Jonathan Benson, Baigrie Davies & Co (IFA); Tom McPhail, Hargreaves Lansdown (IFA); Emma Chamberlain; Patrick O'Brien, HM Revenue & Customs; Mark Hemingway, HBOS banking group; Phil Jacobs, RBR Financial Services; and Colin Jelley, Skandia UK. The following companies helped with facts and figures: Friends Provident, Clerical Medical, Prudential.

And, not least, Paul Holmes, for encouragement, tea, sympathy and vital IT support.

Note: Figures given in the book relate to the 2007–8 tax year unless otherwise indicated.

Introduction

Inheritance tax was once the preserve of the wealthy but it is now affecting the suburbs of middle England as property prices are rising quicker than the annual allowance for tax-free transfers of assets on death. The Government argues that only a minority of estates pay inheritance tax, and it is often said that this is a voluntary tax because there are so many ways to avoid paying it. But millions more families could see their inheritances depleted by this tax in the future. The rate at which it is charged – 40 per cent, the same as higher rate income tax – seems punitive for families where the breadwinners have always been basic rate taxpayers. Whether inheritance tax is voluntary is, perhaps, increasingly debatable. There are many legitimate ways to reduce your potential bill but one of the easiest ways is to give money away. This is not always an option if you do not have a large income or your main asset is the family home.

The increasing unpopularity of inheritance tax is fuelled by the sudden changes in recent years to the rules concerning the tax. The 2006 Budget introduced new taxes on gifts to certain types of popular trusts. Although the effects were chiefly limited to wealthy families, the change was sudden and unexpected and some families have been forced to choose whether to dismantle trusts that were already in place. This policy followed the introduction in 2005 of a fiendishly complicated new tax aimed at deterring people from giving away family homes to avoid inheritance tax whilst continuing to live in them. The result: unexpected tax payments.

The aim of this guide is to explain how inheritance tax works and what the options are for reducing the potential cost for your family. However, inheritance tax and the mechanisms available to reduce it are not necessarily simple. The rules can change suddenly, as we have seen. Individual circumstances change too so it is necessary to review your arrangements regularly. This book is not intended as a substitute for professional advice, which will be necessary for many, if not most, who face a potential bill for inheritance tax. One of the secrets for cutting a potential inheritance tax bill is to start planning early. The sooner you know what you are dealing with, the sooner you can act and it is my intention to help you start planning now.

Budget update

IHT allowances

As a result of the 2007 Budget we now know how much money can be passed on free of inheritance tax (IHT) for every tax year until 2010–11. Chancellor Gordon Brown announced in his 2007 Budget that the allowance, known as the nil rate band or IHT threshold will be £350,000 for that tax year. This follows announcements in the two previous budgets of the nil rate bands for the intervening years. The nil rate band this year, 2007–8, is £300,000, rising to £312,000 for 2008–9 and £325,000 for 2009–10. Estates are currently taxed at 40 per cent above the nil rate band. The Government says that about 35,000 estates will pay IHT in the 2007–8 year.

The increase in the 2010–11 threshold is nearly 7.7 per cent. The Government said that in raising the threshold to £350,000 for 2010–11 it was continuing to provide a fair and targeted system, whereby families know in advance what the tax position is several years ahead. However, the proposed nil rate band for 2010–11was not large enough to satisfy some commentators who believe that, in the future, IHT will fall disproportionately hard on many ordinary homeowning families, forcing them to pay a tax that was once only paid by the wealthiest individuals and estates. For many homeowners, the family property is the main or only asset and were it not for the increase in its price they would not be liable to pay IHT.

Halifax Bank of Scotland (HBOS) has calculated that if the IHT threshold had kept pace with house price increases it would now be £430,000 . After the Budget HBOS expressed disappointment that the threshold had not been increased further, and the accountancy firm, PricewaterhouseCoopers said the Government had missed an opportunity in not doing more to alleviate growing concern over IHT.

If the Budget was disappointing in failing to curtail the scope of IHT, at least it did not spring any nasty surprises, as the 2006 Budget did. Last year's budget included changes to the way gifts into a number of popular trusts were taxed, introducing charges that had not applied before. A pre-budget survey by financial website The Motley Fool found that IHT was one of the three most unpopular taxes. The others were council tax and stamp duty. As one estate-planning lawyer observed, there is little wonder that IHT has 'now become an extremely unpopular tax'.

Pensions

The 2007 Budget also confirmed earlier proposals to introduce new charges on a certain type of pension to prevent people passing funds on free of inheritance tax. The scheme affected is the Alternatively Secured Pension (ASP), which has been available for barely a year. ASPs were introduced primarily for people who have religious objections to annuities that require the purchase of an income for life. Standard pensions require the purchase of an annuity by the age of 75, which uses up all the money in a fund to provide an income through the annuity, but ASPs allow investors to delay buying an annuity beyond 75, leaving a potentially sizeable lump sum in the fund.

The Government feared that ASPs, though designed to provide pensions for a small number of people with specific religious beliefs, might be more widely used as a way to pass money on free of tax. In response to this fear, the Government has introduced rules on the minimum amount of income that must be taken from ASPs, and has established tax charges of up to 70 per cent on 'unused' funds at the time of death.

The Government also announced plans to introduce similar rules on other schemes where it might be possible for funds to be passed on free of inheritance tax. The schemes likely to be affected are specialized ones, but it is clear that the Government is continuing to close loopholes that it thinks might be used to save inheritance tax. The Government has made it plain that it believes pension saving, with the tax relief available on contributions, is not a mechanism to accumulate capital to pass to the next generation free of tax.

Chapter 1

Introduction to inheritance tax

You need this book because:

- more than 2 million homes in Britain are now valued at an amount that could leave the owners' families facing inheritance tax. The figure could be more than 4 million in 2020*
- inheritance tax, which is charged at 40 per cent – the same rate as the highest rate of income tax – can cost tens, even hundreds of thousands of pounds for families of quite modest means
- a house worth £500,000 could leave the owner's estate with a tax bill of £80,000
- husbands and wives could save their families £120,000 at little more than a stroke of a pen by reorganizing their financial affairs
- you can help your children and grandchildren now and legitimately avoid thousands of pounds in inheritance tax
- it is essential to be aware of how you can save tax without upsetting HM Revenue & Customs (HMRC), which is becoming increasingly vigilant about inheritance tax.

So, let's get started. When one 91-year-old pensioner discovered that his family would have to pay a tax bill of £3,000 when he died, he took an unusual approach to the problem. He placed a £500 bet on his own life. At odds of six to one he stood to win £3,000 for his estate if he died before the end of the year.

The pensioner admitted that he placed his bet as a bit of a joke, but the story illustrates the way that inheritance tax (IHT) is beginning to impinge on the lives of people who do not consider themselves wealthy.

*Halifax Bank of Scotland (HBOS) research.

An inheritance tax bill of £3,000 would have been the amount of tax payable in 2005 – the year the pensioner placed his bet – on an estate worth £282,500. This was hardly a fortune at a time when house prices in many parts of the UK were well beyond this figure; in this pensioner's part of England, the south-west, the average house price stood at just under £185,000 at the time he was placing his bet, so if his house was worth a bit more than the average and he also had some savings and investments it is easy to see how his estate might be caught by IHT.

HMRC estimates that around 37,000 estates will have paid IHT in the 2006–7 tax year, representing around six in every 100 deaths. This may not seem a large number of estates, but the number has more than doubled since the 1996–7 tax year.

The first £300,000 of an estate is free of IHT – the amount normally goes up every year and is known as the IHT threshold or nil rate band – and there is no tax when assets pass to a husband or wife, but once an estate tips over the £300,000 mark, tax is charged at 40 per cent of every £1 over that amount.

Traditionally, parents have cherished the prospect that they will be able to pass money on to their children. In Britain, perhaps more than in many other countries, the creation of wealth for the benefit of future generations has become something to aspire to. The children of the aristocracy and landed classes and, later, the families who became wealthy through trade and industrialization were the envy of other sectors of society for their trust funds and the comfort these provided. Some of the nation's best-loved novels are peppered with references to trust funds and inheritances and, in some, entire plots revolve around access to family wealth, or lack of it. It was not until the latter part of the twentieth century that the idea of passing on assets to the next generation became a realistic aspiration for ordinary salaried and wage-earning people. A key factor was the increase in levels of home ownership: around 70 per cent of residences in the UK are owner-occupied. Employees have also accumulated wealth through saving in occupational pension funds and many have also saved through Government-sponsored tax-free savings schemes.

One in 40 people in the UK inherited an average of £17,500 a year between 1996 and 2000, according to statistics released in 2003 by the International Longevity Centre UK. The total amount paid out in inheritances was about £22 billion a year, after tax, over the four-year period. In any one year, around 2.5 per cent of the adult population received an inheritance. The average estate over the 1996–2000 period was worth around £90,000, shared by around five people.

But the acquisition of wealth has also introduced the owners of that wealth to inheritance tax, a form of taxation that previously haunted only the wealthiest of families. Inheritance tax is creeping further and further down the wealth chain, mainly because the value of property has increased much more quickly than the level at which inheritance tax starts to bite into an estate. Many commentators and tax experts have begun to draw attention to this and inheritance tax has become increasingly controversial. Statistics from the Halifax bank (part of the HBOS group), which compiles monthly and annual indices of house price movements, show that house prices have increased by 199 per cent on average since 1995–6. The average price of a home, at £188,623 at the time of writing, is now just under 63 per cent of the IHT threshold of £300,000 compared with 42 per cent a little over a decade ago.

In the 2005 Budget, the Government appeared to acknowledge the gathering discontent about IHT by announcing that it would increase the amounts that people can leave tax-free by more than the traditional annual levels. Between 1997 and 2004, the IHT threshold rose broadly in line with inflation, up to 22 per cent over that period against a 19 per cent rise in the Retail Price Index, according to Halifax Bank of Scotland (HBOS). The threshold rose by 5 per cent in 2005, to £275,000, and by 4 per cent in April 2006 to £285,000. In the 2006 Budget the Government announced small increases for the tax years up to 2009–10 (see table overleaf).

Inheritance tax thresholds: nil rate bands

2005–6	£275,000
2006–7	£285,000
2007–8	£300,000
2008–9	£312,000
2009–10	£325,000
2010–11	£350,000

But even at the new levels, IHT could affect many families. As noted above, the average price of a home in the UK is now nearly 63 per cent of the IHT tax-free allowance. In some parts of the UK the average price of a home is nudging much nearer to the IHT threshold and many homes are of course worth much more than the average in their region (see table below).

Average house prices

North	£145,519
Yorkshire and The Humber	£144,582
North-West	£149,676
East Midlands	£161,930
West Midlands	£173,121
East Anglia	£182,514
South-West	£200,931
South-East	£240,624
Greater London	£287,176
Wales	£159,246
Scotland	£126,639
Northern Ireland	£196,874

Source: HBOS. Fourth quarter 2006.

Inheritance tax: the past

Inheritance tax in one form or another has been part of Britain's taxation system since medieval times. Estate duty was introduced in 1894 by the then Chancellor of the Exchequer, Sir William Harcourt, who had also made the comment, 'We are all socialists now.'

Estate duty, commonly known as death duties, became notorious for its effect on large family fortunes, and in particular on large country estates. In 1949 the tax levy on estates worth £1 million or more (£23 million in today's money) was set at 80 per cent.

Estate duty was succeeded by Capital Transfer Tax in 1975 and this, in turn, was replaced by inheritance tax by Margaret Thatcher's Conservative Government in 1986. From 1987, IHT was charged at a single flat rate of 40 per cent whereas previously there had been a number of tiered rates.

In 1996 the threshold rose by 30 per cent, from £154,000 to £200,000, but then increased in line with inflation until the 2005 Budget, when, as noted above, Chancellor Gordon Brown announced larger than usual increases in the thresholds for the next three years. There will be a 4 per cent rise in the threshold, to £312,000 next year (2008–9), and a 4 per cent rise to £325,000 in the following year.

When the Labour Government came to power in 1997, 500,000 homes were valued at more than £200,000, the threshold for the tax at that time.

The HBOS has calculated that the IHT threshold of £300,000 for 2007–8 would be £460,000 if it had increased in line with average house price inflation since 1995–6. The number of properties valued at more than the threshold stood at an estimated 2.3 million at the beginning of 2007, 12 per cent of all owner-occupied properties. In 2001 only 1.3 million properties, or 7 per cent, were valued at more than the then IHT threshold of £242,000. HBOS states that the IHT threshold has risen by 95 per cent since 1995, against the 199 per cent rise in average house prices.

As inheritance tax is affecting more people, more attention is being paid to ways to avoid it. This has given rise to some complex tax-planning schemes. The Government has taken action to unwind some of these and prevent further avoidance. In 2004 it introduced legislation that put individuals and professional firms under an obligation to notify HMRC of schemes of which the main aim was to avoid IHT. On 6 April 2005 a new form of tax was introduced to clamp down on complex schemes designed to take advantage of loopholes in the rules on giving away assets with the aim of avoiding IHT while continuing to benefit from them. For more information on the significance of this legislation, see page 76. In the 2006 Budget, the Government changed the tax rules on certain types of trusts frequently used for IHT planning, imposing charges on gifts to trust that had not been levied before (see page 76).

Another milestone in the history of inheritance tax was the change introduced in 2005 to the way same-sex couples are treated in relation to the tax. Since December 2005 it has been possible for same-sex couples to register their relationships for legal recognition similar to that acquired by marriage. Where a partnership has been registered there will be no IHT when assets pass from a deceased partner to a survivor.

What the Government earns from inheritance tax

- The Government is collecting around £3.5 billion a year from inheritance tax (at the time of writing). This compares with £1.6 billion raised in 1996–7.
- HBOS says the Government collected £16.4 billion in revenue from IHT in the five years to 2007–8. This was 50 per cent more than the amount raised in the previous five years. The Government's projects are for revenue of £4.1 billion for 2007–8.
- The Institute for Public Policy Research has worked out that inheritance tax raises almost enough to pay for the entire capital budget of the NHS in England.

Who is paying it

Approximately 40 per cent of the estates paying IHT are in London and the south-east of England, according to research conducted by HMRC. HBOS says that the number of estates with a value of less than £500,000 paying IHT rose by 75 per cent over the five years to 2003–4 to 21,750. These estates now account for 71 per cent of all estates paying IHT. In 2003–4, 8 per cent of estates worth less than £500,000 paid IHT, up from only 5 per cent in 1998–9. The average amount paid by estates was £31,393. Estates worth more than £2 million accounted for 19 per cent of IHT revenue in 2003–4, at £526 million. Estates valued at between £500,000 and £1 million generated the most IHT revenue in 2003–4, at £921 million, or 33 per cent of the total, HBOS calculates.

The UK is not the only developed country that levies taxes on inheritance, although several, including Australia, Canada and Italy, do not. The trigger point in the UK, at £300,000, is relatively low compared with the threshold in some other countries, considering that the tax is levied at 40 per cent. But in a number of other European countries, including France and Germany, tax is paid on money passed on by spouses if their estates exceed certain limits, whereas in the UK transfers to spouses are tax-free.

Inheritance tax as a percentage of total tax collected in 2002 was:

USA	1.2
Japan	1.1
France	0.9
UK	0.6
Spain	0.6
Ireland	0.4
Germany	0.3

Many people feel that the mismatch between the rising value of property – the main source of wealth for most families – and the IHT threshold is unfair. Inheritance tax should only be paid by the seriously wealthy, not ordinary working and salaried people, they argue.

But following the re-election of Labour in 2005, it would be unwise to expect major liberalization of inheritance tax rules in the foreseeable future. Indeed, the new tax on larger gifts to certain trusts, announced in 2006, indicated an even tougher approach to IHT by the Government. It would not be safe to assume that a different Government would readily give up this useful source of revenue.

All homeowning families need to have a working knowledge of inheritance tax and how to organize their affairs to avoid it. Ideally, families should also be reviewing their position regularly to see how changes in the value of their assets affect their liability. There is a saying that 'With wealth comes responsibility', and there are good arguments for families to begin to talk openly about inheritance in general, and tax in particular. A frail, elderly parent may be reluctant to get involved in the mechanics of inheritance tax planning and this could create tension within a family. The sooner the issue is faced, the easier it will be for all to deal with it.

IHT is often referred to as a voluntary tax because of the many ways in which it can be avoided or reduced.

There are signs that people are becoming more aware of inheritance tax but research by the Joseph Rowntree Foundation in 2005 found widespread ignorance about exactly how the tax works. Only one in a hundred interviewees was able to answer a series of questions about the tax and payment liabilities correctly. More recent research by Barclay's Bank found that 75 per cent of people qustioned did not know what the current IHT threshold was.

This seems an appropriate point at which to test your knowledge, with a brief quiz incorporating questions that the Rowntree researchers put to interviewees.

1. Do married couples have to pay IHT on assets they give to each other?
2. Does this also apply to unmarried couples?
3. What would the IHT bill be on an estate of £350,000 left by a widow to children?
4. Does it matter whether you make a will?
5. If I give away money will it always be free of IHT?
6. Can I give my house to my children, continue to live in it and save IHT?
7. Do charities pay tax on legacies?
8. Will tax be payable on my tax-free savings: ISAs and PEPs?
9. How long will my family have to pay the tax bill after I die and can the bill be paid out of their inheritance?
10. Can a will be changed after death to save IHT?

You will find the answers to all of the above in the chapters that follow. As a result of finding out about IHT you could save your family and other survivors tens of thousands of pounds.

However, you need to be aware that IHT is a complex form of tax. There are various ways in which you can plan for IHT through making some simple changes to your personal finances; giving money away, for example, is one of the most effective ways to reduce a potential IHT bill. But there are pitfalls, as we will discover later, and you should be prepared to get advice on your own circumstances, even if only to get a second opinion on what you think is the best course of action.

Chapter 2

Inheritance tax and you

The basics: how much and on what

According to IFA Promotion (IFAP), an organization that promotes independent financial advice, the British pay more than £1.6 billion a year more than they need to in inheritance tax. IFAP says that the main sources of this 'waste' are:

- life insurance policies that are not arranged in a way that will ensure they are not taxed. If life insurance is 'written in trust', as it is known, so that the policyholder makes it clear that he or she wants the proceeds to pass to someone else through a simple trust, there will be no tax to pay
- failure by couples to make use of each partner's right to pass on a large amount of their estate, currently £300,000. If spouses pass all their assets to each other, one person's tax-free slice, or nil rate band, is wasted, which could mean that a family pays £120,000 more than necessary in IHT (40 per cent of the nil rate band of £300,000)
- where people die without wills (intestate) and an estate is passed on in a way that results in a larger tax bill than if they had arranged their affairs appropriately before death.

So it is worth getting to grips with IHT.

- First, master the arithmetic. Inheritance tax is charged at 40 per cent on assets that exceed the nil rate band. So, an estate worth £500,000 will have IHT charged on £200,000 (£500,000 minus £300,000) of that amount. At 40 per cent of that sum, the IHT bill will be £80,000.

- There is no inheritance tax to pay when assets pass between husbands and wives. The exception is where one partner has an overseas domicile. 'Domicile', broadly, means an individual's permanent home and is usually his or her country of birth. This is a complex area but it is enough to note at this stage that if you have a spouse who was born abroad you may only be able to pass on £55,000 of assets tax-free.

- Where a man and woman live together as husband and wife but are not legally married, they have no entitlement to this exemption, so IHT is an important consideration for unmarried couples. As outlined in Chapter 1, same-sex couples can pass assets to a surviving partner only if they register their relationship under the Civil Partnership Act 2004, which came into force in December 2005.

- Assets counted towards the value of an estate include property, investments (including assets built up tax-free, such as PEPs and ISAs), bank and building society deposits, the value of personal belongings and valuables and cash.

Many owners of former council-owned properties may now be facing inheritance tax bills. The value of such properties, bought under the right-to-buy scheme introduced in the early days of Margaret Thatcher's Conservative Government in the 1980s, has increased beyond the wildest dreams of former council tenants. In one of the most dramatic examples, an ex-council house in Fulham, one of the smartest parts of London, went on the market in the early months of 2005 priced at £895,000. Five years earlier, the freehold had been bought for £50,000 under the right-to-buy scheme.

Even if the property had not increased since 2005, the potential inheritance tax bill would now be nearly £240,000.

The basics: how to avoid IHT

Make a will

- Making a will is not necessarily a means, on its own, for saving inheritance tax but it can be a key to directing money away from your estate, to a charity or trust, and out of the reach of HMRC.
- There is another way in which the making of a will can help to avoid an IHT bill for your estate. If you die without a will (intestate) your assets will be distributed according to a set legal formula. For married couples this could mean that not all of your money goes automatically to your spouse and, if you have enough money to leave behind, some of it may suffer an IHT charge before it passes to other members of the family. In England and Wales, if your estate is worth more than £125,000 and you have children, only the first £125,000 goes outright to the spouse and the rest is shared with the children. Scotland and Northern Ireland each have their own rules for intestacy.
- Wills are generally advisable for anyone who owns property or other assets, to ensure that their money goes to the people whom they want to inherit it.
- Wills can be used to pass on money in a way that can potentially save your family tens of thousands of pounds in tax. Normally this will be done in conjunction with a trust so that a married couple can make the most of their individual nil rate bands. See the section on trusts (page 41) for more information.

Give money away

- There is a series of exemptions that allow you to give away several thousand pounds a year free of IHT.
- There is no IHT to pay on money left to charity, political parties, housing associations or a variety of national institutions including museums, colleges and universities.
- There is no IHT on gifts made more than seven years before your death. If you die within seven years of making the gift, it will still be tax-free if it is within the nil rate band at that time.

If not, the tax is charged on a sliding scale depending on how long before your death the gift was made. This ranges from 20 per cent of the full rate if you die between six and seven years after making the gift to 80 per cent for gifts made within three to four years of your death.

Get married

If you are living in a heterosexual relationship with a long-term partner and you want that person to inherit your estate, he or she will be liable for IHT if your estate is more than the annual IHT threshold. If you are married, the money can be passed on free of tax. If you are in a same-sex relationship consider registering your union under the Civil Partnership Act. It has been possible to enact civil partnerships since December 2005. The procedure is similar to arranging a marriage through a register office.

Put assets into trust

Trusts do not, on their own, eliminate an IHT liability. In most cases they are, first and foremost, a way of protecting assets for someone else. They are certainly not a way of hiding money from HMRC. But they can be the obvious place to put a gift. Trusts come in various shapes and forms and there have been changes recently to the way IHT is charged on some (see Chapter 9). These changes have reduced the usefulness of trusts for some people but there are other notable ways in which they can be useful for saving IHT:

- you can set up life insurance policies so that the proceeds are put into a trust and will not form part of your estate on death
- money from most pension schemes is held in trust so that the proceeds are free of inheritance tax.
- trusts can be set up so that they only come into being when you die. The typical use here would be by married couples so that they can each take advantage of their personal inheritance

tax allowances. As noted above, there is no IHT on money that passes between husbands and wives on death, but this means that these allowances can be wasted if there is a large estate. It can make sense for parents to put money into trust – through a nil rate band discretionary trust – so that when one dies, an amount equivalent to the nil rate band is passed to children tax-free (see example below). This sort of planning needs care and attention, however, and HMRC is looking closely at the way some of these arrangements have been set up. Trusts are covered in detail in Chapter 9.

Case study

Tom and Jane have an estate worth £600,000 (£300,000 each). There will be no IHT if Tom dies, leaving all his money to Jane. But when Jane dies, £300,000 (£600,000 minus the threshold of £300,000) will be liable to tax, producing a bill of £120,000 (£300,000 at 40 per cent) before the estate passes to the couple's children. However, if Tom dies having made arrangements to put an amount equivalent to the £300,000 into a trust for Jane and the couple's children, this amount will have been removed immediately from the family estate of £600,000. When Jane dies (and let's assume, for the sake of simplicity, that the nil rate band is still £300,000) she will pass on the remaining estate, with a further tax-free slice of £300,000). This leaves the estate free of an IHT liability, a saving to the family of £120,000.

Consider tailor-made IHT schemes

Insurance

- You can take out life insurance to pay lump sums estimated to be sufficient to pay the estimated future IHT bill.
- Term insurance, which pays out on death within set time limits, is used to pay bills that are charged on gifts made within seven years of death.

- Whole-of-life policies, which last for the policyholder's life, are designed to pay out at the time of death, whenever that may be.
- Investment bonds that contain an element of life insurance can be used for IHT planning. There are two main schemes – discounted gift trusts and loan trusts – and they enable the investor to obtain some income from the money they put into the scheme.
- Annuity-based schemes are also marketed by insurance companies; here the investor pays a lump sum for an annuity and this removes a chunk of capital from their estate. The income is used, in part, to pay for insurance to replace the money spent on the annuity when the investor dies.

Other inheritance tax breaks

- Lump sum payments from pension schemes on the death of an employee are normally free of inheritance tax.
- There are allowances for small business people and farmers that entitle them to pass on assets free of IHT.
- The estates of military personnel are free of IHT if the man or woman is killed in war or if injuries from serving during war lead to early death.
- Gifts of art, antiques or other items considered to be of national value can be passed on free of IHT under a special scheme that requires the public to have access to them.

The pitfalls: what you need to know before you start serious planning

Inheritance tax may be brushed aside by tax experts, and even politicians, as a voluntary tax because of the many ways in which it can be legitimately avoided. But this is a complex subject and some arrangements, particularly those relating to trusts, must be implemented with great care.

It is important to realize that to protect your assets from tax on death one of the guiding principles is that you need to divest yourself of wealth while you are alive. But you must consider carefully whether you can really afford to give away money now to save tax later. In an age of steadily increasing longevity many people will want to, or need to, consider using their assets during their lifetime to support themselves or to pay for care in old age. Statistics from the Government Actuary's Department show that a 50-year-old man today can expect to live until he is nearly 80. A woman of the same age can expect to live until she is over 80. Is it really a good idea to live in meagre or even miserable circumstances simply to protect your wealth for future generations?

You may feel quite certain that you can afford to give money away but usually it will be worth talking this through with someone else, and if your plan is to save IHT this should be a competent adviser. Often, saving IHT is not just a matter of taking one or two particular courses of action but of combining various options. This is where professionals earn their money. The information in this book is intended as a guide to help you assess whether you may have an IHT problem and to prepare you to do something about it. After all, the less time you have to spend with an accountant or lawyer going over the mechanics of IHT and the various planning tools, the more you can spend on getting the job done. And you will also need to consider the cost of setting up plans to save inheritance tax and whether these will be justified by the potential savings you may make.

The Government has already acted against some of the more complex forms of planning developed to try to get around IHT rules. Reputable professional advisers will know what can and cannot be achieved comfortably within the law but it is as well to have some knowledge yourself of what the limitations are. You also need to be on your guard against less reputable advisers and to be aware that with rising concern about inheritance tax, financial services companies may be over-eager in their desire to exploit the business opportunities available.

Finally, you need to understand that the rules governing IHT can change from time to time and that once you have an IHT problem, or are close to having one, you need to keep up to date and be prepared to review your situation regularly. Your liability to IHT can fluctuate with changes in the value of your wealth and with changes to the annual IHT allowances. Most people who have owned property over the past decade in Britain need to make themselves aware of the basics of inheritance tax. You may not have a liability now – but what about next year, or the year after?

Scotland and Northern Ireland

The rules relating to IHT are the same in Scotland and Northern Ireland as in England and Wales. That is, there are the same nil rate band allowances, gift allowances, rules for Potentially Exempt Transfers, and relief to assist businesses and family farms. Tax and estate practitioners generally recommend the same methods to assist people in minimizing potential tax bills: programmes of lifetime giving and, if appropriate, the use of trusts.

However, there is an important fact to note. The rules on how estates are passed on if there is no will are different in Scotland and Northern Ireland from those in England and Wales. (See page 35 for more on intestacy and how it can affect inheritance tax bills.)

Another issue in Scotland is that spouses, civil partners and children are entitled to receive certain amounts from a spouse, partner or parent under the forced heirship laws. These cannot be overridden by a will. Families may have to consider how these laws could affect their IHT liability.

There are methods that estate planning experts may recommend to avoid or limit IHT bills as a result of Scotland's rules on how assets are passed on. It may be feasible to transfer assets outside the estate, possibly to trusts. It is also possible for family members to 'disclaim' their rights to receive assets in order to avoid an IHT bill. This must be done within two years of a death.

However, this is an area where Scots families need advice, not least because any attempt to work around the heirship laws to avoid tax would mean that some family members, most likely children, would not inherit.

Do you have an IHT problem?

Your home may be worth more than the current IHT threshold but this does not mean you necessarily have an immediate problem with the tax. If you have a mortgage, and there is no life insurance, the mortgage will be deducted from the value of your estate, along with other debts (see notes below for more detail). But even if you have a large mortgage that reduces the value of your estate, this is not a signal to ignore your potential IHT liability. After all, mortgages are paid off over time, and if the value of your property increases in future your estate could eventually be drawn into IHT.

You are more likely to fall unwittingly into an IHT trap if you live in the south-east of England than in most other parts of the UK. This is where many homes are already above the IHT threshold. Indeed, simply getting a valuation on your home will be a good starting point for working out whether you need to be concerned about IHT.

In a survey of more than 480 towns in England, published by HBOS in 2006, the banking group found that 48, or 10 per cent, had average house prices above the IHT threshold (£285,000). All but two of the towns, Wilmslow in Cheshire and Ilkley in West Yorkshire, were in the south of England.

In a survey of post code districts, HBOS found that the number in England and Wales where the average house price was above the IHT threshold had more than doubled in the five years to the beginning of 2007. The average price in 235 post code districts, 11 per cent of the total, was now higher than the threshold, compared with 117, or 6 per cent, five years earlier. Sales at more than the threshold accounted for a quarter of property sales in a fifth of post code districts across England and Wales.

- In London 41 per cent of boroughs (13 out of 32) had an average house price above the IHT threshold, the highest proportion of any region. Five years earlier, 22 per cent of boroughs (7 out of 32) had an average house price above the threshold. In the south-east 20 per cent of towns (33 out of 169) had an average price above the trigger point for IHT compared with 7 per cent five years before (12 out of 169).

- In the two towns outside the south where house prices breached the IHT threshold, Wilmslow's average was £307,003 and Ilkley's in Yorkshire was £298,703.
- The London boroughs with the highest proportion of sales above the IHT threshold were Kensington and Chelsea (84 per cent), Westminster (72 per cent) and Camden (66 per cent). Sales above the inheritance tax threshold accounted for at least 20 per cent of transactions in 69 per cent (22) of London boroughs over the previous year.
- The towns with the highest percentage of sales above the IHT threshold were Gerrards Cross (82 per cent), Weybridge (68 per cent), Ascot (65 per cent) and Hook (62 per cent). Ilkley in West Yorkshire has the highest proportion (36 per cent) outside the south of England, followed by Wilmslow in Cheshire (33 per cent).
- Sales above the inheritance tax threshold accounted for at least 20 per cent of the total in 22 per cent of English towns over the year to June 2006. More than 80 per cent of these towns were in London and the south-east.
- Sales above the inheritance tax threshold accounted for at least 50 per cent of sales in 18 of the towns and boroughs. All these were in London and the south-east.

Your personal IHT calculator

Before launching into your personal IHT valuation, be aware that you will need to do some preparatory research. For example, if you own shares in a business you will have to get a valuation for your shares. You may also need to get up-to-date valuations for personal possessions and valuables. It is estimated that each UK resident has an average of at least £55,000 of savings and personal possessions that count as 'other assets' for IHT purposes.

Note that the calculation is approximate at this stage. If you think you have an IHT liability looming and you want to do something about it you should see an adviser with expertise in this area. In Chapter 18, we look at finding an adviser. An adviser will carry out a full assessment of your assets and liabilities. You will certainly need to have your own assessment checked, particularly if you have made large gifts recently and you own a business (where there are specific rules to deal with IHT).

Key preliminary points for the calculation

Remember that the calculation is approximate at this stage, to give an indication of whether you need to worry about IHT. The calculator assumes your affairs are relatively straightforward. There are some wrinkles – listed below – in the rules related to calculating IHT that could affect the value of your estate. It is important to be aware of these as an understanding of them will affect a full valuation of your estate and you may or may not want to take them into account when you do your calculation.

- If you have made large gifts to friends or relatives within the past seven years, these should be included as an asset. You can give away £3,000 a year, plus any number of small gifts of up to £250 to individuals who have not already received money within the £3,000 allowance (see page 45 for more details), but larger amounts must be counted as assets as they will be taxable if you die within seven years.
- If you have given something away but continue to use that asset or property, this must be counted as an asset.
- If you have a life interest in a trust, which gives you the right to the income but not the underlying capital, this will be included as an asset and trustees may have to pay a portion of the IHT due on the estate.
- Shares in family businesses may have to be counted as an asset but they may escape IHT altogether, provided they meet criteria intended to ensure that family businesses do not suffer IHT

charges when passed on. If assessing your estate, HMRC would include the value of the business, or shares in it, as an asset and then deduct business relief later in the calculation. The same process is used for farms. But for an approximate valuation of your estate you can ignore the business at this stage. You will need to get advice in any case if you have business assets.

- The value of personal possessions and other valuables, for IHT purposes, will usually be lower than the amount they are insured for, although HMRC will still expect the valuation to be realistic. On death, HMRC will also deduct an amount from your estate for funeral expenses and also for bills due for payment.

- Pensions can normally be excluded as they are usually set up under trust arrangements that exempt them from IHT. But you need to ask the scheme managers whether this is the case.

- Lump sum payments from employers on the death of an employee are normally exempt from inheritance tax and do not have to be counted as part of an estate.

- Life insurance policies written in trust are also exempt. However, life policies that are not written in trust are included as assets; this would normally include policies taken out to repay mortgages. These may be assigned automatically to a mortgage lender.

- Couples should list their assets separately and where items such as property are owned jointly count half the total value for each person.

- For married couples, where there is no IHT to be paid on the first death, this may not seem particularly relevant. But as IHT could be payable on the second death, it is important to get an idea of the total value of assets held by husband and wife.

- Where a couple is unmarried, it is vital to count assets separately as there is no IHT exemption for money passed from one partner to another. As noted earlier, same-sex couples who have registered a relationship since December 2005 will be treated in the same way as a married couple, but unmarried heterosexual couples are vulnerable to IHT where their individual estates are large enough to breach the nil rate band.

- Where you own assets jointly with someone else but are not married – a long-term partner, brother, sister or friend – HMRC will normally reduce the value of each individual's share by, typically, 10 per cent. So a £400,000 home owned half and half by an unmarried couple comprising a brother and a sister, for example, would give each an asset value of £180,000 (£200,000 less 10 per cent).

Your personal IHT valuation

Step 1
List your assets:

- your home
- second homes and rental properties (including those abroad)
- car, boat
- savings in bank and/or building society accounts
- ISAs, PEPs
- shares, unit trusts
- personal effects such as jewellery
- household contents including antiques and other values
- life insurance policies – excluding those written in trust
- pensions, unless written in trust
- business, unless you know it will qualify for IHT relief.

Total assets: £

Step 2
List debts and liabilities:

- mortgages
- personal loans
- credit cards.

Total debts and liabilities: £

Deduct debts and liabilities from assets

TOTAL NET ASSETS: £

Step 3
Deduct the nil rate band of £300,000.

Step 4
Now calculate tax at 40 per cent.

How a married couple's asset statement might look

Assets	Martin £	Maud £
Family home: total value £500,000	250,000	250,000
Holiday home	100,000	
House contents and personal possessions	25,000	25,000
Bank or building society ISAs, PEPs and TESSAs	20,000	20,000
Premium Bonds	1,000	
Life insurance for mortgage	50,000	50,000
Car	10,000	5,000
Personal effects, collectables, jewellery	7,000	2,000
Totals	**463,000**	**352,000**
Minus		
Liabilities: what you owe		
Mortgage	50,000	50,000
Bank, car, other loans		5,000
Credit cards	1,000	
Net value of estates	412,000	297,000

Tax tip

If Martin or Maud dies there will be no IHT to pay on assets passed to the surviving partner even though the value of each estate is over the nil rate band. But, assuming no changes in the value of their estates, when the second partner dies the combined estate will be worth £709,000. This is £409,000 more than the nil rate band and tax at 40 per cent would be £163,600. There are steps that Martin and Maud could consider to reduce their bill and these will be described in the following chapters.

Tax trap

While pension funds can normally be disregarded in a calculation of assets, don't get the impression they can be used as a tax dodge. If someone decided not to draw a pension from a pension fund, in the expectation that survivors would inherit a tax-free lump sum, there could be a tax bill.

Case studies

Marian is in her mid-30s, single and has a flat in north London valued at £300,000. Marian earns a good salary from her job in advertising and has a mortgage of £150,000 on her property. She has savings of £5,000, household and personal possessions worth about £30,000, and a car provided with her job. Since Marian has no children or other dependants, she has decided not to buy life insurance to repay her mortgage, so if she dies now her estate will be reduced substantially by the value of her loan. At £300,000, her property is worth no more than the nil rate band, and when the mortgage is deducted the net value of her home is £150,000. When her £5,000 of savings and £30,000 of possessions are added, her estate comes to a net total of only £185,000 and there are no immediate concerns for her about IHT.

*   *   *

Mary and Ken, both retired, own a house in Cornwall that has recently been valued at £275,000. They have no other savings except for a small personal pension fund of £30,000 that Ken saved into during the latter years of his working life and a separate pension from a former employer. They have savings of £20,000, some of which is in PEPs and ISAs. Ken collects model trains and was surprised, when he valued his collection recently, to discover that it was worth nearly £10,000.

Mary and Ken do not have to count Ken's pensions in their estate as both are written in trust – as is the case with most personal and occupational pension schemes – but they do need to take into account their savings and Ken's model collection. Altogether, their estate is worth £305,000. If either of them dies there will be no inheritance tax to pay, because they are married, but the bill on the estate could eventually be £2,000. This is worked out as follows: the total value of their estate is £305,000. The first £300,000 is exempt from IHT, leaving £5,000. Tax at 40 per cent is £2,000.

* * *

David and Eleanor are married and live in west London in a comfortable home, which they believe is worth approximately £500,000 and on which they have a £100,000 mortgage. As they have children and want the family home to be protected, each has life insurance equivalent to the amount of the mortgage to cover the whole debt if either of them dies. The policies will pay out to the surviving partner on the death of the first to pay off the mortgage, so they are counted as part of the estate. The couple also have savings of £5,000 but no other investments apart from savings in their pensions. Their estate is therefore worth £505,000. As they are married, there will be no inheritance tax to pay on the estate when the first partner dies. But when the survivor dies, and assuming no changes in the value of their assets, there will be a bill to pay on £505,000 minus the nil rate band of £300,000, which works out at £205,000. At 40 per cent the potential IHT liability for Eleanor and David is £82,000.

* * *

Michael and Samantha have been living together for 15 years and are not married. They are both self-employed and work from home, Michael as a management consultant and Samantha as an interior design consultant. They own a home in a part of London where house prices have skyrocketed in recent years. They are fortunate enough to have been able to repay their mortgage, which was only ever a fraction of the property's current value, in full. It is now valued at around £700,000. Michael has savings of £40,000 and Samantha £20,000. They estimate that the contents of their home are probably worth around £70,000 as they have some valuable furniture. They each have cars that might fetch £10,000 if sold.

Michael's estate is valued at £396,500: £315,000 for his share of the couple's house (after taking account of the 10 per cent discount because he and Samantha are not married), £40,000 in savings, £31,500 for his share of the contents of the home (£35,000 minus 10 per cent) and £10,000 for his car. When the nil rate band of £300,000 is deducted, Michael is left with £111,500 that is potentially liable for IHT. At 40 per cent the bill would be £38,600.

Samantha's estate is worth £376,500, £20,000 less than Michael's because she has half the amount of savings that he has. Her assets come to a total of £376,500, which, when the nil rate band is deducted, leaves £76,500 and a potential IHT liability of £30,600.

Michael and Samantha own their property jointly and have made wills to leave each other their assets. But as they are not married they cannot pass their estates to each other without triggering IHT bills.

*   *   *

Simon and Madeleine have been living together for several years and have a home in south-east London worth £320,000. Simon has no savings of his own and does not own a car but has an interest in art and owns paintings worth £10,000. He also has £2,000 outstanding on credit cards. The couple's furniture and household possessions are worth approximately £40,000, they think. Madeleine has £5,000 in savings accounts and a car worth about £2,000 on which there is still £1,000 of borrowing to pay. The couple have a mortgage of £100,000. Each of them has £50,000 of life insurance to pay off their share of the mortgage if they die. They have no children so they have not felt it necessary to insure the full value of the loan, on the assumption that the surviving partner would continue to work and pay off his or her half of the loan.

How much tax will you pay?

Estate £	Amount taxable £	IHT at 40 per cent £	IHT as per cent of estate
300,000	Nil	Nil	Nil
350,000	50,000	20,000	5.7
400,000	100,000	40,000	10.0
450,000	150,000	60,000	13.3
500,000	200,000	80,000	16.0
550,000	250,000	100,000	18.8
600,000	300,000	120,000	20.0
650,000	350,000	140,000	21.5
700,000	400,000	160,000	22.8
750,000	450,000	180,000	24.0
800,000	500,000	200,000	25.0
850,000	550,000	220,000	25.8
900,000	600,000	240,000	26.6
950,000	650,000	260,000	27.3
1,000,000	700,000	280,000	28.0

Note: The tax-free allowance for the 2008–9 tax year, starting 6 April 2008, will be £312,000. So, to work out the bill on an estate after that date, deduct the new allowance from the net value of the estate, to find the taxable amount, then apply tax at 40 per cent. An estate worth £500,000, for example, will have a taxable value of £188,000. At 40 per cent the bill will be £75,200.

Simon's estate is valued by halving the value of the couple's jointly owned home, a share of £160,000, minus 10 per cent because they are not married, making £144,000, then adding £18,000 for household contents (half of £40,000 minus 10 per cent), adding on the value of his paintings (£10,000), and then deducting his £2,000 of credit card debt. Because there is life insurance to pay off Simon's half share of the mortgage, the debt is not deducted from the calculation. Simon's estate is worth £170,000, £130,000 below the IHT threshold.

Madeleine's calculation goes as follows: a half share in the house of £144,000, plus £18,000 in household contents, £5,000 in savings, plus £1,000 for her car. This comes to £168,000, also well within the nil rate band. However, if Simon and Madeleine plan to leave their assets to each other there could still be IHT to pay on the death of the second survivor.

Chapter 3

What to do about your IHT bill

Let's assume you have discovered to your horror – or delight – that you are worth rather more than you thought and that your family might, indeed, have to pay inheritance tax on the money you leave them.

Now is the time to work through the various options available for reducing your potential bill, or avoiding a bill completely.

Don't start giving money away indiscriminately. While gifts can save thousands in inheritance tax, you also need to consider how much you need to keep in order to maintain your lifestyle. You also need to know the rules on saving inheritance tax in order to avoid falling into expensive traps.

In approximate order of importance – relevance will depend on individual circumstances – these are the main ways to deal with a potential IHT bill.

- Make a will or review the one you have already.
- If married, consider leaving assets up to your nil rate band to your children, through a trust.
- Assess your legal ties to your long-term partner: it may be time to get married.
- Look at life insurance to cover any IHT bill that might be payable.
- Give money away now, using tax-free exemptions.
- Make gifts to charity now or through your will.
- Think about putting money into trust – particularly life insurance policies, where appropriate.
- If you have a business or farm, investigate the special arrangements available for passing on these assets.

- Consider how you might invest in future to build assets that do not count towards an IHT bill.
- Find out about insurance-linked schemes tailor-made to reduce or eliminate IHT bills.

Chapter 4

Where there's a will

If you die without leaving a will you have died 'intestate'. The law dictates who your money will be passed to and this may not match your wishes. The only exception is where assets are owned jointly. This is the case with many homes owned by married couples – the legal definition is joint tenants rather than tenants in common – and also joint bank and savings accounts.

According to research in 2005 by the Joseph Rowntree Foundation, more than half the adult population has not made a will. Among people aged 80 and over, the figure rises to 84 per cent. More home-owners than non-owners have wills, but even among those with property one in four has not yet made a will.

Husbands and wives may assume that if one of them dies their estate passes automatically to the other. They would be wrong. In England and Wales, if the estate is worth more than £125,000 it will be shared between the spouse and children, if there are any, or the spouse and other relatives if there are no children. The rules are different in Scotland and Northern Ireland, but here also, where there are children, the estate must be shared between them and the spouse.

Note that same-sex couples who have registered their relationships as civil partnerships have rights to inherit from their partners if they die intestate. See below for summaries of intestacy.

In June 2005 the Government began a review of the rules governing intestacy in England and Wales. The Department for Constitutional Affairs (DCA) estimated that there were up to 9,000 cases each year where a surviving spouse did not receive all of the husband's or wife's estate, and in 4,000 of these cases the family home may have had to be sold to release money to pass on to children.

Dying intestate could also leave your family with an unexpected inheritance tax bill. In the past, the distribution of an estate under the intestacy laws probably landed relatively few families with unexpected tax bills. But now that the rising value of so many homes has catapulted ordinary families into the inheritance tax bracket, it is becoming more important for families to be aware of the consequences of intestacy. The average house price, at the time of writing, was a little under £190,000 against the £125,000 that goes automatically to a spouse under the intestacy laws in England and Wales. Just over a decade ago, when the current intestacy limits were set, 90 per cent of estates were worth less than £125,000 and 98 per cent were worth less than £200,000, but the proportions now are about 60 per cent and 80 per cent respectively.

The DCA has proposed that the amounts that can be passed on automatically to a spouse should rise to £350,000 if there are children involved and £650,000 where there are no children. In Scotland, the amounts that can be passed on were changed in June 2005.

At present, if a couple own assets worth more than £125,000 (in England and Wales) and they have children the spouse will receive the first £125,000 and a life interest in half of the remainder, which means they can receive income from the asset but not the asset itself; that is left in trust for children. The surviving spouse also gets the dead husband's or wife's personal effects but the rest of the estate goes to the children.

Dying intestate in England and Wales

- Husbands, wives and civil partners get £125,000 plus personal possessions.
- If there are children the spouse or civil partner gets £125,000, personal possessions and the right to income from half of the rest. The children receive the other half.

- If there are no children but there are parents who are still alive, the spouse or civil partner gets the first £200,000 of the estate plus half the balance, and the rest goes to the parents.
- If there are no parents alive but there are brothers or sisters, they get what remains after the spouse or civil partner has taken the personal effects, the first £200,000 and the half of the remainder.
- If there are no parents or brothers or sisters the spouse or civil partner receives everything.
- If you are not married or in a civil partnership and there are no children the estate goes to your parents or, if they are not alive, to brothers and sisters.
- If you are not married but have children the estate is shared between them.

Dying intestate in Scotland

- Where there are children, the spouse gets the family home up to a value of £300,000, furniture and household effects to a value of £24,000 and cash of up to £42,000. The spouse also has the right to a third of the rest that is 'moveable', which generally means investments rather than property. The children also get a third of the remaining moveable estate and the rest goes to other relatives.
- Where there are no children, the spouse gets the family home to £300,000, household furniture and effects to £24,000 and cash up to £75,000. The spouse has a right to half the moveable estate that remains and the rest goes to other relatives.
- Civil partners are entitled to half the moveable estate if there are no children. If there are children, the partner gets a third of the moveable estate.

Dying intestate in Northern Ireland

- Where there are children, spouses and civil partners get the first £125,000 and all personal effects. Any amount over this is shared with the children.
- Where there are no children, husbands, wives and civil partners get the first £200,000, personal effects and half of the rest. Anything over this goes to parents, brothers and sisters.
- If there are children but no spouse or civil partner, the estate is shared between the children.

Can you spot the risk for inheritance from a potential inheritance tax bill? Look at the following example of what could happen.

Harold dies leaving assets of £1,000,000, including £10,000 of personal possessions. The first £125,000, plus the personal possessions, will go to his wife Helena, leaving £865,000. Of this £865,000, half (£432,500) goes to Helena, for her to retain an interest in while she is alive. All of this money passes free of inheritance tax because of the spouse's IHT exemption. But the remaining £432,500 will go to the children. Remember that the nil rate band is £300,000, which, when deducted from this amount, leaves £132,500 – on which there will be an inheritance tax bill of £53,000 (40 per cent of £132,500). If Harold had left everything to Helena there would have been no IHT for the family to pay now. As we have seen already, this sort of arrangement can leave a family open to an unnecessarily large bill later, on the death of the second spouse, but as we will also see later there are ways in which this can be dealt with by planning ahead.

The purpose of the example above is to show why it is not safe either to assume that intestacy will ensure that your money goes to the person whom you would want to benefit, or that it poses no threat from IHT.

There is another way to look at the effects of intestacy on inheritance tax. If assets pass to children, your IHT allowance will reduce or eliminate the bill, whereas otherwise the allowance will probably be lost (because it cannot be used when the remaining spouse dies). And admittedly, a husband or wife still needs to have quite a substantial personal estate (and possibly to be the whole, rather than joint, owner of a valuable property) for this to be a problem. But families need, increasingly, to be aware of the risk of intestacy.

It is likely to cost more to wind up the affairs of an intestate individual than those of someone who has set out his or her wishes in a will.

Even worse than an unexpected IHT bill would be a shortage of ready cash in the family to pay it. If a dead husband's estate was made up almost entirely of the family home, the family would have to find cash to pay HMRC. At worst, where a large IHT bill was due on a large and valuable home, a family might be faced with the prospect of having to sell in order to pay the bill. This may be an extreme example, but it drives home the point about intestacy.

If the rules on intestacy are changed in England and Wales as the Government proposes, the risk of an inheritance tax problem will be reduced for many families. But this should not stop anyone from making a will.

In Scotland, increases in 2005 in the amounts that can be passed on through intestacy will have assisted some families in avoiding bills. Nevertheless, the spouse only receives a third of moveable assets where there are children, so if there is a large portfolio of investments the estate that passes to the children can exceed the nil rate band.

Where there's no will there still may be a way

There may be a way around intestacy. The law allows for wills to be changed up to two years after someone dies. Families can also arrange to have inheritances reorganized if a parent dies intestate. This is known as a 'deed of variation' and can be a useful way of rearranging someone's affairs to avoid IHT. There are rules about how this is done, of course – and it will be necessary to see a solicitor to ensure the procedure is carried out correctly – not least that all those who stood to benefit under the original will must agree to the change. So, if you can vary wills, or – effectively – create them where they did not exist, why worry about making one? Apart from the stress that families may suffer in having to create or reorganize a will after a death, there are lingering doubts about whether deeds of variation will be permitted in future. There has already been one attempt to get rid of them, by the Conservative Government in 1989, which relented only after a prominent campaign by the legal profession. One of the arguments put forward at the time was that deeds of variation were, in effect, a safety valve for families whose elderly or ill relatives had been unable, or unwilling, to sort out their affairs before death.

Case study

When Peter dies, his will – not updated for 20 years – leaves every-thing to his widow Janice. He did not want to change the will as he wanted to be sure that Janice would have enough capital to pay for nursing care if she needed it in future. Janice's accountant suggests she makes a deed of variation to leave the nil rate band to a trust from which she and the couple's children will benefit. This means that Peter's IHT-free allowance is saved but Janice can continue to benefit from the money if she needs to. The potential saving for the family is £120,000.

Using wills to deal with inheritance tax

You can use your will to avoid inheritance tax in two main ways:

- giving money: gifts to charity are always free of IHT

- for married couples, creating trusts to use the tax-free nil rate band that would otherwise be lost if on the first death everything were to pass to the spouse.

Chapter 5

Giving to charity

This is one of the most straightforward ways to avoid, or reduce, an IHT bill, quite apart from the general social benefits derived from donations. The list of organizations that can receive money from wills tax-free is surprisingly large and extends even to registered housing associations and political parties. In the case of political parties they must have at least two MPs who gained their seats at the most recent general election or one MP and at least 150,000 votes, in total, at the last general election.

Another way to look at gifts to charities through wills is that, given that the money would have been taxable otherwise at the IHT rate, you are boosting the donation by 40 per cent. This effectively makes a sum of £1,000 worth the equivalent of £1,670.

Among Britain's ten largest charities, legacies make up approximately 40 per cent of income. There are any number of charitable organizations crying out for funds and in some cases they will even subsidize the cost. You should be aware that if there is any question that the charity put pressure on you to leave it money in your will, the legacy could be challenged by other people who benefit from your estate. But established, reputable charities will know the rules in this area. You can also give money to other 'worthy causes': the full list includes universities in the UK, Government departments, local authorities, the Countryside Council for Wales, Scottish National Heritage, the National Trust and National Trust for Scotland, the National Art Collections Fund (the Art Fund), the National Gallery, the British Museum and the national museums of Scotland, Ulster and Wales, libraries that provide teaching and research facilities for a UK university, and even certain health service bodies.

The scheme that allows items of historical and artistic importance to be gifted to the nation in return for having the inheritance bill on them wiped out is having a significant impact on Britain's store of treasures available to the general public.

Paintings and items of historical value worth £13 million were saved for the nation as a result of gifts accepted by the Treasury during the 2004–5 tax year. The gifts included Italian Renaissance paintings, works by William Blake and a variety of documents and papers of national significance, including letters by the English poet Kathleen Raine, who died in 2003. The Renaissance paintings were part of the estate of the 6th Marquess of Bath, who died in 1992. Tax that would otherwise have been due on them was believed to come to more than £3 million.

Case study

Catherine is a widow aged 84. She has no children and her estate is valued at £450,000 including a house worth about £300,000. She manages quite comfortably on the state pension and a pension from her late husband's former employer. Catherine has no close family to whom she would like to leave assets. Apart from a few small gifts she wants to leave all her money to an animal charity. She updates her will to make sure that it sets out her wishes. By leaving the bulk of her assets to charity there is a tax saving on her estate of about £66,000 (£450,000 minus nil rate band of £300,000 = £150,000 at 40 per cent = £60,000).

You do not need to stipulate in a will how much you want to give to a specific charity; you can state that the balance of your estate goes to a charity or charities after other bequests. Charities Aid Foundation, an organization that promotes and organizes tax-free giving to charities, runs a legacy account that would allow your executors – the individuals responsible for making sure your will is executed in the manner you set down – to nominate charities.

Tax tip

If your estate does not yet exceed the nil rate band of £300,000 you should consider making your charitable donations while still alive. This way you can take advantage of Gift Aid tax relief, which boosts donations by the equivalent of income tax.

Chapter 6

Nil rate band trusts

This is an unattractive piece of jargon but one that married couples need to become familiar with if they are considering ways to save inheritance tax. The benefit they derive from being able to pass assets to each other tax-free has a downside: one nil rate band is lost on the death of the first spouse unless specific arrangements are made to use it. This usually means – as briefly described already – giving an amount away, equivalent to the nil rate band, usually to children, into a trust that comes into being on the death of the first partner.

Same-sex couples who register their relationships under the Civil Partnership legislation, which came into effect in December 2005, should also consider how they might make the best use of inheritance tax planning techniques. These couples gain the right, if they register their partnerships, to pass on assets to each other free of tax. So where there are larger estates it may be appropriate to organize their affairs so that they are not wasting their IHT nil rate bands.

Setting up nil rate band trusts is simple, in theory, particularly where liquid-asset investments can be put into them. It is even possible to buy an off-the-shelf IHT nil rate band trust from at least one insurance company, although the choice of investment is restricted to an investment bond.

But nil rate band trusts can be complex in practice – particularly in relation to family homes – mainly because the arrangements must satisfy HMRC that they are not a sham undertaken simply to avoid IHT and to get around the rules on gifts with reservation.

HMRC has recently begun to question the validity of some of these arrangements, particularly when used to avoid IHT on a family home. At the time of writing there was a strong body of opinion among senior solicitors and accountants specializing in inheritance tax that nil rate band trusts must be set up in a certain way in order to be bulletproof. After all, the potential tax saving for just one family would be £120,000; it is not hard to see why HMRC would be looking closely at this area.

Now, more than ever, it is vital to get advice from a professional who knows what he or she is doing here. We will look in Chapter 18 at how to find an IHT adviser but first a description of what specialists feel is necessary to make these arrangements 'safe'.

If you want to pass an amount equivalent to the nil rate band to someone other than a spouse or registered partner, you could simply make a bequest in your will. But more often than not there will not be enough liquid assets to make such an outright gift. Often the money that is in danger of being taxed is tied up in a family home and the surviving spouse would still need to live in the property.

But the problem here is that HMRC might argue that, in effect, the surviving spouse still owns all of the property outright and that therefore it should still be counted as part of his or her estate. So, back to square one: when the second partner dies, the full value of the estate is taxed instead of the original total minus the nil rate band.

Tax-planning professionals are increasingly recommending that these arrangements be made so that the nil rate band value becomes a debt – through an IOU – from the surviving spouse to the trust that is set up on the death of the first partner. The surviving partner retains the asset in his or her name and when that partner dies, the trust set up on the first death claims back the debt, taking the money out of the second partner's estate.

One of the main aims of the arrangement should be that it allows the surviving spouse flexibility over his or her use of the asset. The trust itself should be reviewed regularly and administered correctly in order for HMRC to be satisfied that it is genuine.

There is another important point to bear in mind here. To set up an arrangement like this, each partner must own a share of the property in his or her own right. If the couple's home is owned on a joint tenancy basis the deceased partner's share automatically becomes the property of the survivor. Couples must own their homes as tenants in common to set up a nil rate trust and this may mean changing the way they hold their property.

Tax-planning professionals report that it is not unusual to see clients for whom one or more aspects of nil rate band planning – done, presumably, by ill-informed or sloppy advisers – has been executed incorrectly. If you have made such arrangements some time ago it may be worthwhile having them checked for a second opinion to make sure they fit with the latest thinking in this area and that the basic paperwork is in order.

Another factor to consider is the cost of setting up such arrangements compared with the saving in IHT (see page 120).

Case study

Patricia and Neil made wills where each instructed that amounts equal to the nil rate band at the time of death should go into trust, with the remainder going to the surviving spouse. Their home was worth about £570,000 so they expected that on the death of the second partner the estate would have no IHT to pay. But the couple sought advice about their finances from an accountant, who reviewed the arrangement for IHT and found that they still owned their house as joint tenants rather than tenants in common. The accountant obtained a 'notice of severance' to set the ownership of the property up as tenants in common, and hence Patricia and Neil are on course to save at least £108,000 in IHT (£570,000 minus £300,000 = £270,000 at 40 per cent = £108,000).

Chapter 7

Gifts that will save inheritance tax

For most people, one of the most useful ways to deal with an inheritance tax problem is to regularly give small amounts of money away. Giving away large sums is not, of course, advisable if you might need that money to maintain a comfortable life. But the Government allows for quite reasonable sums to be given each year, the sort of money that parents might, in any case, hand over to children. Knowing about the gift allowances might concentrate your mind if you have not quite got round to writing that cheque.

Giving money away might sound like the simplest act in the world but, as is so often the case in tax matters, it can become complicated. There are strict limits on the amount that can be given without triggering a tax bill. Here are some basic principles to bear in mind:

- start early – the more you give away in small amounts the easier and cheaper it will be to reduce the size of your estate. But it cannot be stressed too strongly that you should not give money away in a panic about IHT. Think carefully, consult with your family and see a professional adviser before deciding whether you really can afford to start handing over assets to others
- there is a series of allowances that you can use to give away several thousand pounds a year
- when you have exhausted these limits, gifts from your estate will still avoid tax if you survive for seven years
- if you give away assets other than cash you might be landed with a capital gains tax (CGT) bill

- if you give money to companies or some trusts (see page 54) there may be a bill to pay when you make the gift
- you cannot give money or assets away, continue to use or benefit from them and expect your estate to escape a tax bill (see also page 58).

How much, to whom, and when?

Wedding gifts

- Parents can give up to £5,000 each to their children on marriage, including stepchildren and adopted children.
- Grandparents can give up to £2,500 each to grandchildren.
- Anyone can give up to £1,000 to any friend or relative as a wedding present.

Other gifts

- You can give up to £3,000 a year and, if you do not give all of this away in one year, you can add the difference to next year's gift allowance. But you can only carry forward the allowance for one year. After that it is lost. For these purposes, a year means a tax year, which runs from 6 April one year ending on 5 April the next.
- In addition to the £3,000 exemption, you can also give up to £250 each to as many other people as you like. The money can be handed over in small amounts gradually over the year but the total to that individual cannot exceed £250 if you want it to qualify for relief from IHT. Husbands and wives can give away £250 a year in this way, enhancing the family's ability to pass on assets free of IHT.
- Maintenance payments for the support of your family are not affected by IHT. In particular, this includes payments to a spouse, ex-spouse, dependent relatives and children under 18 or in full-time education.
- The exemption for gifts to your children to pay for education

Tax tips

- When you give away cash, keep a record of the amount and the date of the gift.
- The £3,000 annual exemption can be used to 'mop up' the first portion of a larger amount. Any balance may qualify under other provisions for relief from IHT – more of which a little later.
- You cannot give one person £3,000 plus £250 in one year.
- Don't underestimate the usefulness of the gift exemptions. For every £3,000 given away the potential saving for survivors is £1,200. Over five years that works out at £6,000, over ten years, £12,000, and over 20 years the saving will be £24,000.
- Stakeholder pensions can be bought for a child, so can be a useful way for a grandparent to give away money to grandchildren; the purchase of the stakeholder plan counts as a tax-free gift. Up to £2,808 a year can be put into a stakeholder pension for someone else, but with tax relief this is topped up to £3,600. A grandparent who decides to invest the full amount for a grandchild from birth to the age of 18 – and where the regular payments could count as normal gifts out of income and therefore be free of IHT for the estate – could build the child a pension fund of more than £200,000 at the age of 65, in today's money.
- Child Trust Funds (CTFs), the Government-backed savings scheme for children, that provides vouchers of £250 to all children born on or after 1 September 2002, with a further £250 at the age of seven, may be useful for grandparents who want to give money to grandchildren. Up to £100 a month and £1,200 a year can be saved in CTFs and grandparents could use their IHT gift exemptions to boost contributions. The returns on CTFs will depend on what they invest in but one provider has calculated that £100 a month saved over 18 years could grow to more than £37,000.

or training may be increasingly useful to families who want to help their children through school and university and simultaneously reduce the size of family assets.

Creative use of the gift allowances can help significantly to reduce the size of an estate.

The gift allowance rules allow for a certain amount of flexibility in the timing of gifts, so that if you can afford to give away only a little one year but more the next, you can do so. You could give away up to £6,000 in one year if you gave nothing in the previous one. A husband and wife could give away £12,000; assuming that all of this would otherwise be subject to inheritance tax at 40 per cent, they would save their survivors £4,800 in tax.

A family that wanted to get really creative with the gift exemption, and where neither parent had used the previous year's £3,000 tax exemption, could give away £12,000 (£6,000 each) on the last day of one tax year, 5 April, and a further £6,000 (£3,000 each) the next day, the start of the new tax year. This would make a total of £18,000 over 48 hours, saving £7,200 in tax.

Even more could be given away if the parents could also afford to give up to £250 each away to various family members and friends, remembering, of course, that someone who has received £3,000 cannot be given £250 on top.

It is also worth noting that you can make gifts under more than one of the categories. For example, you could give a child who is getting married a total of £8,000: £5,000 under the wedding gift allowance of £5,000 and £3,000 under the £3,000 general exemption. Parents could give £10,000 (£5,000 each) to a child getting married plus £6,000 (£3,000 each).

Giving away money from your regular income

If you have an income that is beyond what you need to live and maintain your usual standard of living there is potential to give away as much as you like. This is in addition to the gift exemptions outlined earlier; this tax break is all about income, not capital.

The crucial aspect of this is that the amount you are giving

Tax tip

To prove that a gift out of income is regular and habitual you should put the details in writing. This could be a letter to the person you plan to pay regularly or, for example, if you intend to pay school fees, writing to the school to confirm your intention to take responsibility for the fees.

You should also keep a record of your income and expenditure to prove, if necessary, on your death that gifts out of your regular income were made from money surplus to day-to-day requirements.

---

must be part of your regular, habitual spending, and comes from income, not capital, and that, when the amount is given away, you still have enough to live on without reducing the standard of living to which you are accustomed.

Examples of this type of gift would be simply giving a child an allowance, to help with educational costs perhaps, paying school fees for a child or other relative, or regularly helping a less well-off individual to maintain his or her life. An example of the latter could be supplementing the income of an ageing parent.

Case study

Simone and Sigmund are in their late sixties, and they have a son and a daughter. Their son is due to marry soon and their daughter has three children.

They decide the time is right to start giving some of their capital to their family. Sigmund gives each of the grandchildren £250. Simone gives their son £5,000 as a wedding present and another £5,000 to help him set up home. Sigmund has a sister who is disabled and gives her £3,000 towards the cost of her care. Sigmund feels he has done well in life but has a brother who is short of money and decides to give him £1,000 a year out of his income.

There is no tax to pay on any of the gifts because the £250 gifts to the grandchildren are tax-free and the wedding gift is tax-free under the wedding gift exemption. Simone's second gift of £5,000 to the couple's son is tax-free because she uses this year's £3,000 gift allowance and can also use £2,000 of last year's unused allowance. Sigmund's gift to his disabled sister counts as family maintenance and his regular gifts to his brother will count as regular gifts out of income. (Sigmund has done a personal budget to show that he can afford to make these payments regularly without reducing his standard of living.)

Tax tip

Your estate may, potentially, be saved more inheritance tax than you think when you give away valuable items. The value of a gift for inheritance tax purposes is measured by the loss in value to your estate. This can have some interesting consequences if you give away something that loses value as a direct consequence of your action. For example, if you own a pair of valuable ornaments that are more valuable as a pair than as single items your estate will have lost more value than simply half the combined value of the pair.

A pair of vases worth £500,000 might be worth £200,000 each if sold separately. So, if you give one away the loss to your estate will be £500,000 (the original value) minus £200,000 (the value of the remaining vase), which is £300,000. This will be the loss to your estate and the amount by which your gift will be valued if you die.

Similarly, if you give away shares in a company and as a result you lose control over it, any shares that you keep will now be worth much less than when part of the original holding.

Other types of gifts that can save IHT

Beyond all the exemptions and allowances already listed you can give away as much as you like and there will be no IHT bill if you live for seven years. That is the simple bit.

Matters become more complicated if you do not survive for seven years. You also need a working knowledge of the types of gifts that you might make while alive that would suffer an immediate tax charge.

Gifts that are tax-free if you live for seven years

Known in the inheritance tax world as PETs (Potentially Exempt Transfers), these can be vital companions for someone who wants to give away money to avoid inheritance tax. They are useful for people who can afford to give away more than the amounts allowed each year tax-free by HMRC and that are detailed above.

PETs would be an even more useful tool if you could predict your date of death: provided you live for seven years after making a gift there will be no tax to pay.

If you die within seven years, and your gifts until the time of death add up to more than the nil rate band at that time, the tax on any excess may be reduced from the standard rate of 40 per cent, on a sliding scale depending on the number of years that have passed since the gift was made.

This 'taper relief' cuts the normal rate of IHT from 40 per cent on gifts made between seven and three years before death (see table below). If the gift was made more than three years before death but within four years the bill will be reduced by 20 per cent of 40 per cent (8 per cent), making an actual bill of 32 per cent.

There is no reduction on gifts made within three years of death.

Years since gift made	Reduction in tax (per cent)	Rate on the gift (per cent)
0–3	0	40
3–4	20	32
4–5	40	24
5–6	60	16
6–7	80	8

You do not have to tell HMRC about a PET at the time you make it but you should keep a record because the people responsible for dealing with your affairs if you die will have to produce records for HMRC and these records will be vital for working out the total tax bill on your estate. If your estate is large enough for you to be considering this type of giving you will need to take professional advice anyway.

If you die having made a series of PETs, tax is worked out by listing them in chronological order, adding them up and deducting the running total from the nil rate band for inheritance tax applicable in the year that you died. Bear in mind, of course, the fact that you could have given away £3,000 a year anyway with no tax strings attached: such gifts will be disregarded (or deducted from a larger gift) when HMRC comes to tot up the bill.

Because taper relief is only applied once PETs have been set against the nil rate band it is really only useful to estates where very large sums have been given away.

Case study

Gwendoline dies in April 2007, having left gifts to several friends in the years before her death. She had already used her basic annual gift exemptions when these were made. In 1999, six years before her death, she gave £150,000 to Harry. This is well within the current nil rate band of £300,000, so there is no tax to pay on the gift. But the gift of £150,000 leaves only £150,000 of nil rate band (£300,000 minus £150,000 = £150,000) to set against the next gift that Gwendoline made, of £200,000, to friend Sophie in May 2001. The running total of gifts now exceeds the nil rate band by £50,000. IHT, at the standard rate, on the gift to Sophie would be 40 per cent of that amount (£20,000), but because Gwendoline made the gift four years before she died the tax can be reduced by taper relief. For gifts made between four and five years before death the charge is reduced by 40 per cent. So, 40 per cent of £20,000 is £8,000, and the tax bill on Sophie's gift works out at £18,000.

Gwendoline also made a smaller gift than her previous ones to another friend two years before she died. The amount was £70,000, but because all of Gwendoline's nil rate band was now used up on the previous gifts and because there was no taper relief available, the gift having been made within three years of her death, the tax bill on this was £28,000.

The way that PETs are taxed can produce anomalies and apparent unfairness in the way tax is charged on an estate. When the value of a series of gifts exceeds the nil rate band at death, inheritance tax becomes chargeable. If you make a series of small gifts in the years just before your date of death, but have previously made a large gift, say, six years before your death, that large gift will have eaten up your nil rate band, leading to a larger bill on the small gifts than might otherwise have been the case.

Footing the bill for tax on PETs

If a tax charge arises on a PET because the donor has died within seven years of handing over the money, HMRC will seek payment from the person who received the gift. It may return to the estate for payment if it cannot get the money from the recipient, so the potential liability will need to be spelled out to the people to whom you are giving money.

You could take out life insurance to provide for payment of IHT that might become due on a PET. The aim would be to take out cover that would last for seven years and reduce over that time to cover the reduction in tax that might be due from taper relief.

The individual who makes the gift could pay for the insurance, although be aware that the cost of the insurance itself could be counted as a gift. You may be able to pay for insurance out of your normal everyday expenditure (in which case there will be no tax) or take the cost out of your yearly £3,000 gift exemption. Arrange with the insurance company to have the policy written in trust so that it goes directly to the person whom you want to benefit (the one who has received the gift), rather than to you and your estate, where it could add to your IHT charges. Another option is for the person who is receiving the gift to take out insurance on the life of the donor.

Normally, the tax on PETs has to be paid within six months of the end of the month in which the donor dies, and interest will be charged if the bill is paid late.

Case study

John has an estate worth £500,000 when he dies. But five years before his death he gave £200,000 to his son. If John had lived for seven years after making the gift to his son, there would be no tax to pay, but because he dies within five years of making the gift it is added back into the value of his estate. HMRC sets it against his nil rate band of £300,000, leaving only £100,000 to set against the £500,000 estate. The gift is not taxed because it comes within the nil rate band, but the remaining £400,000 of the estate is taxed, which, at a rate of 40 per cent, presents the estate with a bill of £160,000.

Taper relief is irrelevant because the gift is within John's nil rate band.

Beneficiaries of John's estate might be aggrieved that while no tax is charged retrospectively on the gift made to his son, they will see the value of their inheritance reduced by a proportionately larger amount because the gift is set against the nil rate band. Had John survived for seven years the tax on his estate would have been £80,000 (40 per cent of the £200,000 taxable after deduction of the nil rate band of £300,000).

Tax tip
Start giving money away early, if you can afford it.

However, it is also worth noting that you have to give away substantial amounts of money to be concerned about the gift becoming taxable, even if you do die within seven years. This is because the gift, along with any others made within the last seven years, will have to take you over the nil rate band before tax becomes a problem. This does not mean that the rest of your estate will not face a tax bill but, depending on the size of your gifts, an understanding of the way PETs are charged could enable you to rest easy about the recipient of your generosity having to pay tax. Remember also that even when tax does become payable it will be on the amount by which your gifts have exceeded the nil rate band, not by the full amount. Taking all this together, it is not surprising that HMRC says that IHT is not charged on many gifts.

Gifts that are taxable immediately

Some gifts may suffer an inheritance tax charge immediately. This applies to gifts made to companies and gifts to several types of trusts. Gifts to trusts by individuals are more common than gifts to companies. In the 2006 Budget the rules on the taxation of gifts into trusts changed. The changes were complex but meant, essentially, that two types of trust – accumulation and maintenance trusts (A&Ms) and interest in possession trusts (IIPs) – that had previously had the potential to save families substantial amounts in inheritance tax, were brought into line with the rules on discretionary trusts where gifts were already, potentially, taxable. Gifts to IIPs and A&Ms had been treated as PETs (potentially exempt transfers) with no tax to pay provided the donor survived for seven years. Now the system is broadly the same as that for discretionary trusts. See also the next chapter for more about trusts. This type of immediately taxable gift is known as a chargeable lifetime transfer. Gifts of more than the nil rate band suffer a 20 per cent tax share, then 6 per cent every 10 years, plus further charges when money is paid out.

Case study

Anthea sets up a discretionary trust for her grandchildren at the end of 2006, when the nil rate band for IHT was £285,000, and puts £100,000 into it. Anthea has made annual gifts to family and friends totalling £3,000 each year for several years and these are tax-free, but this substantial sum is in addition to those sums. However, because the £100,000 is well within her nil rate band for the year, there is still no tax to pay. The following year she gives another £250,000 (again, in addition to her annual gift of £3,000) to the trust so that her cumulative total is now £350,000. The nil rate band is now £300,000, so £50,000 is now taxable at 20 per cent, which is £10,000 if borne by the trust.

If you are giving money to a company or trust and there is a tax charge to pay, the bill can be paid by you, the giver, or by the recipient company or trust.

This raises a complication in calculating the tax. If the company or trust receiving the money pays the tax it is known as a gross gift. If you, the giver, pay the tax it is known as a net gift. If the giver pays, the amount that goes in tax is itself counted as part of the gift, which means that, when working out whether any tax is due, you will need to calculate tax at a rate of 25 per cent of the running total of immediately chargeable gifts, minus the current nil rate band. This takes account of the fact that the tax paid has the effect of inflating the gift: to achieve the value of the gift you want to make (to take in the tax) you need to gross up the value in this way to include the tax, then find the charge on the total.

If you make a gross gift, leaving the recipient to pay the tax, the amount that ends up in the hands of the recipient will be less than if you made a net gift and paid the tax yourself.

Looking at the example of Anthea above, if she had borne the cost of the tax herself as a gift paid net of tax, she would work out the tax on her £250,000 gift by adding this to her previous year's gift of £100,000 to get her a running total of £350,000. Again, when deducted from the nil rate band the amount that is taxable is £50,000, but at 25 per cent the tax works out at £12,500.

Looked at another way, a net gift, where the tax is subject to the grossing up calculation, will usually lead to a higher tax bill than a gift where the recipient pays the tax.

As you can see, taxation of gifts can become complex. If you are making regular gifts to a trust you will, presumably, already have consulted professionals to set up the trust and they should assist you in keeping track of your tax position.

You can take out life insurance to protect the recipients of lifetime transfers – as well as PETs – from tax bills that would arise if you died within seven years of making the gift. As the giver, you could take out a policy, but the cost of the premiums would themselves count towards the total value of the gift. Alternatively, the recipients could take out a policy on the giver's life and pay the premiums.

Tax trap

Be aware that if you are giving away non-cash assets you may have to pay capital gains tax on the gift if it has increased substantially in value since you acquired it. CGT is charged at whatever is your highest rate of income tax. However, there is an annual exemption that normally increases each year and this may protect you. You will need to take possible CGT implications into account if giving away items of value, and you will need advice on this.

Tax tip

If you have been given something that has fallen in value and there is a potential tax bill because the giver has not survived for seven years, you will be able to subtract the fall in value from the original value of the gift.

How gifts will be taxed when you die

If you are leaving money to friends and family you may want to give some thought to the way IHT will be charged on those gifts. If you leave instructions that the balance of your estate, after a number of other gifts have been made, is to go to a spouse and/or charities – who are exempt from IHT – they could receive considerably less than you intended unless you make specific arrangements for the way tax is charged on other gifts. This could happen where you make a number of gifts and do not instruct that tax is to be paid by the recipient. If you make gifts without leaving such instructions, it will usually be assumed by HMRC that tax is to be paid by the estate. This results in a calculation similar to the grossing up mechanism that can occur with gifts made while one is alive to discretionary trusts and companies. The assumption is that the tax is part of the gift. Making a lot of gifts that are taxed this way could lead to higher tax bills than otherwise intended, to be met from the residue of the estate (the amount left after specific gifts have been made). Those named as beneficiaries of the residue – which could be a husband, wife or charity – could, at worst, see their inheritance whittled away to nothing to pay tax on grossed up gifts.

As with many other aspects of planning inheritances, this is an area where your solicitor or accountant should be able to advise and forecast potential tax bills. It is something you should raise if he or she does not.

Chapter 8

Gifts that aren't gifts

Gifts with reservation

These are gifts of the 'have your cake and eat it' variety. They are the type of gift that most people facing an inheritance tax problem would like to make, but are frowned on by HMRC. If you give something away and continue to benefit from it, the full value of the item will have to be included in the value of your estate. HMRC's definition of a gift with reservation is where:

- the recipient does not occupy or enjoy bona fide possession of the gift
- the donor still retains or enjoys a significant benefit from the gift.

If a reservation on a gift ends during the lifetime of the donor, the gift is treated as a PET at that time. The gift is subject to IHT if the donor dies within seven years of the time that the PET is deemed to have been made. If the reservation still exists when the donor dies, the property is treated as part of the donor's estate and taxed accordingly.

HMRC also considers that if the donor occupies or enjoys the asset but pays a genuine market price or rent for doing so, the gift may not be treated as a gift with reservation. The rules surrounding gifts with reservation are particularly relevant to inheritance tax planning related to a family home and to assets where the donor wants to continue to receive a benefit, typically an income.

HMRC has given some guidance on the circumstances in which it considers a gift not to be one with reservation:

- If the donor occupies or enjoys the asset but pays a market price or rent to do so, the gift may not be treated as a gift with reservation.
- If a house is given to a relative and the donor needs later to live in the house, he or she may do so if the following conditions are met: the recipient of the gift is related to the donor or the donor's spouse; and the donor needs to occupy the house because of unforeseen infirmity, or in order to be cared for in old age.

There is also guidance on other circumstances in which a gift will or will not qualify for IHT relief.

If you give your house to a son or daughter you may stay there for up to two weeks a year without the gift becoming one with reservation. But if you stay in the house most weekends it will be considered a gift with reservation.

The status of gifts can also change over time. If you live rent-free in a house given to a child, for two years, the house will be a taxable asset – if you die – within that period. But if you start to pay rent after the two years the 'reservation' will cease and, provided you live for seven years from the time you paid the first rent, there will be no tax to pay. Conversely, if you start off by paying rent but later stop, or the rent does not keep pace with market rates, the gift will become taxable.

At first glance the rules are clear but there are various shades of grey. The conflict between the desire to avoid inheritance tax while continuing to benefit from property and other assets while alive has given rise to some creative schemes by accountants and financial advisers. It has also produced some skirmishes between taxpayers and HMRC. The Government has recently tightened up in this area, with new legislation on what it calls 'pre-owned assets' introduced in April 2005. This is explained in more detail on page 76.

Case study

Rita and Richard have a home worth about £650,000. They have made wills to use both of their nil rate bands, but there will still be a potential IHT bill of about £20,000 and that liability is rising with the increasing price of property in their area. A few years ago their daughter Clare came to live with them after her marriage broke up. The family expect Clare to live with them permanently now. Their accountant has suggested that they give away a third of the property to Clare. As the gift would be outright and Clare will live with them this would not be regarded as a gift with reservation by HMRC. Each of the three, Rita, Richard and Clare, have estates worth less than the nil rate band, so Clare can expect eventually to inherit without paying IHT.

Chapter 9

More about trusts

Perhaps the most important point to note about trusts and inheritance tax is that this area has become a minefield for families and their advisers. Some trusts are relatively simple and the way that they are used in conjunction with inheritance tax is straightforward.

The 2006 Budget introduced changes to the taxation of some trusts that took financial planners by surprise. The result has been to make certain types of trust less attractive for inheritance tax planning by wealthier families. This may not be the last time that the rules on trusts change in relation to inheritance tax. There was speculation, at the time of updating this book, that there could be new rules on the way for taxing bare trusts.

Why so much change? Trusts do not automatically eliminate a tax bill. The terminology surrounding them can be confusing but the basic premise is that money is being given to someone else for safekeeping on behalf of another person. Tax is a secondary issue. But, as we have seen in earlier chapters, giving money away while you are alive is one of the main ways to avoid a large charge on your assets when you die. If you want to protect money for a future generation and want to give it away now it is natural that tax-saving allowances will be used in conjunction with trusts. The changes in the 2006 Budget seem to be a clear signal that the Government believes that trusts are being used too widely to avoid potential IHT bills. The original, and highly complex proposals that the Government produced in the 2006 Budget were greeted by storms of protest from solicitors and accountants. As a result the plans were modified before they were introduced as legislation. Accountants and advisers are still familiarizing themselves with the new system, and the full implications of its effects may not be known for some time.

One of the results, according to one specialist solicitor, is that clients have become extremely wary about IHT planning. Those most likely to be affected are families who want to give away more than the prevailing nil rate band (£300,000 this year). But it has become more important than ever to get specialist professional advice on basic IHT planning with trusts.

Before explaining the changes from the 2006 Budget, however, it is important to note, that some types of trust are useful to people of relatively modest means to protect their assets from IHT.

As we saw when looking at the types of asset that must be counted as part of your estate, life insurance and pensions – two of the most common and valuable forms of asset for most ordinary people – can be written in trust. The death benefits from pensions are generally held in trust arrangements as a matter of course. When you die, the money you own within the pension goes to the trustees, who decide who should receive the proceeds. Usually this will be a husband or wife but can also be someone nominated by you – a long-term partner, for example. Payments from the pension may provide a regular income on your death but will usually also include the 'death in service' benefit – lump sums payable to a spouse or nominated individual. Because of the trust arrangements, payments from pensions are normally untouched by IHT.

However, there are new rules on the way that will ensure that a new type of pension, the Alternatively Secured Pension (ASP), cannot be used to avoid large IHT bills. The ASP, introduced in April 2006, allows people aged 75 or more to avoid buying annuities with their funds. The Government feared that people would store funds in these pensions, take a minimum income while alive and pass money on avoiding IHT charges. There are to be new rules introduced to ensure that a minimum income is drawn and there will be a 70 per cent tax charge on any money still left in the fund unless it goes to a dependent or charity.

Life insurance policies that you purchase independently of

your employment can also be put into trust arrangements so that the people whom you want to benefit can receive the money free of IHT. Another advantage of having a policy written in trust is that money can be paid out quickly when the policyholder dies. A death certificate is all that is required, rather than the policy being caught up in the formalities of probate. To have a life insurance policy written in trust it is normally necessary simply to complete a form provided by the insurer, although solicitors say that it is important to ensure that the company has provided the correct form; you may need to clarify this with the insurers and if necessary take advice. Trust arrangements for life insurance and most pensions have the potential to benefit millions of people. However, financial advisers report that a surprisingly large number of people fail to put life insurance policies into trust, thus potentially landing their families with unnecessary IHT bills.

Trusts used by married couples and civil partners to ensure that one IHT nil rate band is not 'wasted' – as described earlier in this guide – should escape IHT on the money put into them on the death of the individual whose will sets them up. As noted already, these arrangements must be set up carefully, particularly if they are used to save a share in the family home. There is more information on this in Chapter 12 (page 76).

Giving money away does not necessarily mean that you need to put it into trust. Don't get carried away with the idea that a trust per se will bypass an inheritance tax liability. As we have already seen, there are a number of annual exemptions that allow for money to be passed on free of tax and beyond these there is the PET regime that, potentially, allows for larger gifts to be tax free if you survive for seven years, or charged at a lower rate than normal if you die within seven years.

Trusts for larger gifts and the 2006 Budget

There are several other types of trust that can be used when you want to give money away but maintain some control over its use. All are more complex arrangements where a solicitor – and probably a specialist in estate planning – will usually be needed to draw up the relevant documents, where the trust may need to be registered with HMRC and where you will need to appoint trustees. Normally you can be a trustee yourself and you might also appoint a solicitor or accountant. You will need specialist advice to make sure that the arrangement you are setting up is right for you. Tax is only one of the issues here; you will probably also be considering how assets will be divided within a family.

Trusts used for more complex types of IHT planning come in a variety of forms. With a discretionary trust the benefits, which can be capital and/or income, are paid to the beneficiaries according to the directions – and at the discretion – of the trustees. With an interest-in-possession trust, income – interest, dividends from shares, rent or the use of a property – must go to a specific, named beneficiary. A husband might leave assets to his wife to draw a benefit, such as an income, without being able to use the capital, which passes to their children. Interest-in-possession trusts tend to be less flexible than discretionary trusts because they are specific from the outset about who is to benefit from the money held in trust and about how the person is to benefit.

With an accumulation and maintenance trust, traditionally used to pass money on to children and grandchildren, income and/or capital can be used to help support a child, teenager or young adult – to pay school fees, for example – or any income from the trust can be reinvested to accumulate. Accumulation and maintenance trusts can last for a maximum of 25 years.

An interest-in-possession trust gives one person a right to benefit from an asset while he or she is alive but the asset then passes to someone else. Or, a widow might get the right to live in a house during her life but the property ultimately passes to the children.

Until the 2006 Budget, payments into interest-in-possession and accumulation and maintenance trusts were treated differently to those into discretionary trusts. They were treated as PETs, so as long as the donor survived for seven years there was no tax to pay. Now they are treated in the same way as discretionary trusts, with charges at 20 per cent on gifts that are over the current nil rate band, 6 per cent every 10 years and up to 6 per cent when the assets are paid out. On an accumulation and maintenance trust the only way to avoid the charge is if the families are prepared to give their children control of their money at age 18. If money is handed over between the ages of 18 and 25 there are charges on a sliding scale.

At the time of writing, tax and estate planning specialists were, as noted earlier, still working out how clients would be affected. There was also an option to change the terms of a trust by April 2008 to qualify under the old IHT gift rules. Families who think they have trust arrangements that could be affected should seek advice if the adviser who originally set up the arrangement has not been in touch.

Advisers do not believe that many families will want to hand full control of money in trust funds to children at 18. They also believe that the changed tax status for accumulation and maintenance trusts will reduce their attractions as a way for families to give money and save IHT.

However, it is worth noting that the new tax charge only affects gifts over the nil rate band, currently £300,000. Tax on gifts over this into one of the affected trusts will still be less, potentially, than a full IHT charge. Advisers say that it can still be worthwhile setting up trusts to take gifts of sums less than the nil rate band, although you will need to put in less than the actual band amount, growth in the fund could tip it over the nil rate band in future years creating a tax charge on the tenth anniversary. But considering that a couple can each put gifts close to the value of their nil rate bands into trust, there is still scope to use trusts for gift and IHT planning.

Some advisers expect less use of trusts and more use of the standard allowances for giving money away regularly, including the PET regime. The recent changes have added to the complexities and uncertainties that can accompany IHT planning for families with substantial assets and make it more important than ever to obtain advice (see Chapter 18, page 116).

At the time of writing, financial advisers expected accumulation and maintenance trusts to become less popular than in the past because of the tax changes. Greater use would be made of discretionary trusts (see below).

Bare trusts

A bare trust is a simple trust arrangement normally used to give money to children. This money is then held until they are 18. At that age a child has the right to take control of the assets held in the trust. Grandparents who want to hand money on to children often use these trusts. When parents give money to a child in a bare trust they should be aware that if the income is more than £100 a year they will have to pay income tax on this. But income from gifts from other friends and relatives will be counted as the child's and, provided the child's total income is below their annual personal allowance, there will be no tax to pay. Any assets sold within the fund, and which result in a capital gain, will also be set against the child's annual capital gains allowances, which means that in most cases there will be no tax bill. A possible disadvantage of bare trusts is that the adults who give money to a child in this way have no control over what happens to it when the child reaches 18.

For IHT purposes, if your gift to a bare trust is within your annual tax-free allowance (see page 4) it will not suffer any IHT. At the time of writing, larger gifts into bare trusts were treated as PETs – nothing to pay if the donor survives for seven years. But HMRC has signalled its intention to look at the tax status of bare trusts. Its concern is that some are being used as quasi-discretionary trusts and should be taxed as such (as indeed interest-in-possession and accumulation and maintenance trusts now are).

More on discretionary trusts

Discretionary trusts are likely to become more widely used now that accumulation and maintenance trusts no longer have favoured tax treatment.

There are several variations on the discretionary trust. As already noted, the common thread is that the trustees have the discretion over how and when money is paid out to beneficiaries. This is what gives them their flexibility – within certain limits laid down by the person who sets up the trust.

In a general discretionary trust it is possible to pay benefits to a group of individuals without having to name them specifically. They are often used by people who want to create funds to benefit children and/or grandchildren, even those not yet born. The beneficiaries do not, as with an accumulation and maintenance trust, have a specific entitlement to any benefits from the trust; this is at the discretion of the trustees. A discretionary trust can come into being at the time that the giver of the assets (the settlor) dies. You can state in a will that you want to set up a trust on your death to receive assets for children or grandchildren, a spouse or a civil partner. This is a common form of inheritance tax planning; a 'discretionary will trust' is created through the wording of a will to receive assets for children or grandchildren. Discretionary trusts are normally the type used when couples set up nil rate band trusts to accept assets or a share in a property up to the IHT nil rate band. You can also arrange your will so that your executors decide whether to set up a trust on your death, depending on how much money you leave, the tax position of your estate at the time of your death and who is to receive the money.

Charitable trusts

You could set up your own fund to benefit charity by creating a discretionary trust while you are still alive or arranging for the trust to come into effect when you die. You might do this if you want a specific cause to benefit where there is no specific charity already, or where you prefer to retain control over how the funds are spent. You will need specialist advice to set one up.

Trusts are also used in conjunction with packaged schemes linked to insurance and investment products (see Chapter 13, page 94).

Jargon unscrambled

In the world of trusts, the settlor is the person or persons (or a company) who gives assets to put into trust. These assets can be cash, property or shares. In Scotland the settlor is known as the truster or grantor. The beneficiaries are the individuals (usually at least two) or entities (which could be companies, charities or others) who will benefit from the assets in the trust. But the beneficiaries are not necessarily the owners of the property. The legal owners and safe keepers of the assets are the trustees. Someone who stands to benefit from the trust can also be a trustee, as can the settlor (although for the settlor there can be tax complications) or the individual or individuals who give money to the trust.

Tax trap

Do check the status of your pension(s) for IHT problems. Modern personal pensions set up since July 1988 are usually written in trust, and provided you have filled out a form making it clear who should receive the benefits, any payments from the scheme on your death should be free of IHT. But some pensions taken out before July 1988 – generally known as retirement annuity contracts – were not set up under trust arrangements as a matter of course. It should be possible to put old contracts into trust, but act sooner rather than later, as HMRC might question the arrangement if you die soon after making the change.

Chapter 10

Family businesses and farms

Giving away family businesses and farms

There are special rules to protect family businesses and farms from inheritance tax. Provided various conditions are met families should be able to pass on their businesses free of IHT. There are exceptions, though. Businesses that deal in shares, land and other investments do not qualify and nor do those that exist simply to make or hold investments. Businesses involved in letting out properties are also excluded from special IHT exemptions unless they are involved in furnished holiday lettings.

Broadly speaking, the rules on inheritance tax for businesses and farms ensure that there will be no IHT to pay (i.e. there will be 100 per cent relief, as HMRC describes it) during the owner's lifetime or on death if the assets are:

- a business that has been running for at least two years, or an interest in a sole trader's business or in a partnership
- unquoted shares in a company or shares listed on the Alternative Investment Market (AIM).

There will be IHT at 50 per cent to pay on:

- shares in companies traded on the London Stock Exchange where you have a controlling holding (5 per cent or more)
- land, buildings, equipment and machinery used for a business that you control. This also applies to partnerships

- land, buildings and machinery used for businesses held in trust for you.

On the face of it IHT is straightforward for families with businesses and farms.

For example, an estate worth £1 million might generate no inheritance tax at all if it consists largely of a family business left to a son or daughter with any cash, property or other assets left to a spouse. But there are traps and pitfalls as well as ways to minimize tax. It is preferable, if possible, to leave businesses to children rather than to a husband or wife; in the latter case, the asset would have been free of IHT anyway because of the IHT exemption for spouses. Debts on a family business will be deducted from its value for the IHT calculation (as with personal assets), but because there will be no IHT anyway on the estate, it may be worth paying off business debts with cash or other assets that would be subject to IHT elsewhere in the estate.

Families who own businesses must take advice on inheritance tax. Hopefully their advisers will raise the subject with them if they know enough about their clients to know that there could be an IHT liability looming.

Here are examples of complexities that can arise:

- if there is a lot of cash in a business account, HMRC may decide that this has been placed there deliberately to avoid IHT
- if business premises once used for trading are now let out, this can reduce IHT relief
- while it is possible to give away your business or farm before you die, tax may become payable if you do not survive for seven years. There could also be a charge if the person to whom you gave the business has sold it. The exception to the latter rule is where the person has not reinvested the proceeds of the sale in a new business or farm. Again, this is an area where you should not do anything without professional advice
- if a business owns assets that are not used primarily or only for

the business to do its work – expensive 'trophy' cars, for example, or a yacht – the IHT relief is reduced in proportion to the amount of use the business actually makes of those assets

- there will not be full relief if the business is in the process of being sold. But with the correct advice a group of partners could organize the purchase so as to have the option but not an obligation to buy
- if you sell a business and die the following day there may be no IHT relief – and you might also trigger a capital gains tax bill that would not have arisen if the assets had been passed on at the time of death. But if you sell in return for unquoted shares in a trading company you may protect the relief. Therefore, owners of family businesses need to have a strategy for dealing with the disposal or passing on of their valuable assets
- if you hold some of the assets used by a company, you could consider transferring them to the company so that there is full IHT relief rather than just 50 per cent relief. In addition you may also be able to reduce the value of your personal estate this way
- if you have a large amount of money tied up in a home you could raise a mortgage on it and invest the cash in a family business or unquoted shares. If you hold the shares for two years and meet the other conditions that apply, business relief will remove the IHT that would have been payable on the home. This sort of manoeuvre is not without risks, however, and because there are conditions to meet it should not be undertaken without advice.

When passing on a family farm no IHT is payable on the 'agricultural' value of the land and buildings, although this may not be the same as the market value. Neither stock nor equipment used on the farm qualify for IHT relief, although they may qualify for business relief. As with a business, there is a two-year rule: you must have occupied the farm for two years or more or have owned it for seven years. Full relief (100 per cent) is only available if you have farmed the land yourself; relief at 50 per cent is given if it was let to someone else to farm.

Chapter 11

Inheritance tax and the unmarried couple

Broadcaster Jenni Murray, presenter of Radio 4's Woman's Hour, married her partner and father of the couple's two teenage sons after 22 years of unmarried bliss. The reason? Inheritance tax.

Murray told a national newspaper that the decision had been made reluctantly as she did not want to marry and was also concerned that the move might damage her relationship. It didn't, but the couple felt they had no choice but to formalize their union. A financial adviser had nagged them, she said, because if one of them died the other would be hit by a big inheritance bill. As the main breadwinner Murray worried that if she died her partner would have to sell the family home to pay the bill.

By marrying, Murray and her partner acquired the right to pass on assets to each other free of IHT. Many other unmarried couples may be unaware of how they would be affected if one of them died.

Research by the Halifax suggests that as many as 200,000 people in co-habiting relationships are living in homes valued at more than the IHT nil rate band. There is considerable misunderstanding among co-habiting couples about their legal rights. Many couples believe that they acquire the legal rights and protections of a married couple after they have lived together for a certain length of time. This concept tends to be referred to as a 'common-law' partnership but, in law, there is no such thing. There is some protection for couples who have lived together for two years or more and where one co-habitee dies without a will (see box overleaf), but apart from this, co-habiting couples need to make their own arrangements to protect themselves.

If you are in a long-term relationship but are not married, and you have property or other valuable assets, you need to pay particular attention to how inheritance tax could affect you. Living as a couple while remaining unmarried is not the preserve of the young these days. People in middle age may choose to live this way for a time before committing themselves to marriage.

If you are not married to your partner you cannot pass assets on to that person free of inheritance tax. In December 2005 new legislation, the Civil Partnership Act 2004, was introduced, allowing same-sex couples in the UK to register their relationships and to acquire virtually the same legal rights as married heterosexual couples. Through separate legislation this includes the right to pass on assets free of inheritance tax. Hence, same-sex couples who register their relationships as civil partnerships will need to look at inheritance tax planning in the same way as married couples do now. This could include making use of both nil rate band allowances by leaving money to individuals other than partners, as outlined earlier in the book.

It is vital for heterosexual co-habiting couples to realize that it will not be possible for them to register their relationships as civil partnerships. For them, marriage remains the only option if they want the full legal protection that marriage provides for partners whose finances are interlinked. Those who have assets of their own worth £285,000 or near that amount must be aware that their estate could be liable to an inheritance tax bill. If they leave a share of a valuable property to a partner this could, at worst, mean that the partner comes under pressure to sell the property to pay the inheritance tax. Unmarried couples in this position should consider how they would cope with an inheritance tax bill under these circumstances. One of the cheapest and most suitable options – unless they decide it is time to get married – would be life insurance to pay a lump sum to cover a potential IHT bill.

If one partner in a co-habiting couple dies without making a will the surviving partner does not automatically receive a portion of the estate as under the intestacy laws. If a property is held jointly it will pass to the surviving partner but if not – and it is held on a tenants in common basis – assets will be distributed according to the rules of intestacy. This will provide protection for children from the relationship but could put the partner in an extremely awkward position.

The exception is where the relationship has existed for at least two years before the death or where the surviving partner was supported by the deceased. Here you may be able to claim under the Inheritance (Provision for Family and Dependants) Act 1975. You need to make the claim within six months of the death and you will need to make it through a court, so legal advice will be necessary.

Case study

Tom is a highly paid banker who is living with Martha, a social worker. They become concerned about the effect that inheritance tax could have on their estate and decide to get married. They set a date, but in the meantime they come across their dream home, which costs £800,000 and which they buy from the proceeds of Tom's flat, supplemented by a mortgage to be paid by Tom. In the eyes of HMRC Tom has made a gift of half of the share of the property to Martha and, were he to die, there would be an inheritance tax problem because the house was bought before they married; there would be no spouse's exemption from tax. If Tom were to die within seven years the potential bill would be £40,000: tax at 40 per cent on half the value of the property at £400,000, less the nil rate band of £300,000 (£400,000 minus £300,000 = £100,000 at 40 per cent).

Tom and Martha would have avoided this problem if they had bought the property in Tom's name and transferred it to joint names after they married. If Martha takes on responsibility for the mortgage now there is a potential liability for stamp duty – on the notional purchase of her share.

Chapter 12

Inheritance tax and the family home

You love your home, but it is causing you a tax headache. It has increased in value so much in recent years that it could land your children with a tax bill when you die.

You are not alone. Many, if not most, of the people now concerned about IHT are in that position because of the value of their homes. The problem is clear: giving away money is one of the most effective ways to reduce the size of an IHT bill, but you can't strip the roof off your house to achieve the same result. Homeowners need to find some way to offload the value without falling foul of one of the cardinal rules of IHT tax planning: you can't give something away with strings attached and expect your estate to save tax.

There are options, of which more shortly, but first it is important to be aware that the law affecting IHT and family homes has recently been changed. The Government shows every sign of being ready to act at the earliest opportunity against attempts to get around the gift with reservation rules.

Pre-owned assets tax

A new piece of tax jargon has come into common use among accountants, solicitors and members of the public who are concerned about inheritance tax: the pre-owned assets tax, also known as the POA tax or POAT. This is a new form of taxation introduced on 6 April 2005 to deter people from attempting to get around the rules on gifts with reservation. In the eyes of the

Government, too many people were trying to have their cake and eat it with inheritance tax by devising and using complex schemes aimed at making it appear that they had given away assets that, in reality, they were still using in some way.

The new regime does not affect people who want to release equity from their homes through a commercial equity release scheme. But it is causing headaches for families who have made individual arrangements with family members, for instance where a parent sells or gives shares in the home to children or even gives money to a child and moves in with him or her later.

The POAT imposes income tax charges on the benefit people are deemed to have derived from assets they have given away but continue to have an interest in – living in a house, for example. In the case of property the charge is on the estimated market rent for the property, at the taxpayer's highest rate (the highest rate payable by that individual) and for items such as paintings it is 5 per cent of the market value.

So, a house worth £500,000, with a projected rental value of £25,000 a year, will produce an income tax bill of £10,000 a year for a higher-rate (40 per cent) taxpayer (£25,000 at 40 per cent = £10,000). A painting worth £100,000 will have a notional value of 5 per cent (£5,000), on which the annual income tax charge would be £2,000 for a higher-rate taxpayer.

There will be no bill, however, if the notional benefit is not more than £5,000 a year. Going on market rates for rentals, this would correspond to a property worth about £100,000. But if the benefit is worth just £1 over the £5,000 threshold, tax is applied to the full amount, not just the amount by which the benefit exceeds the threshold. If the person who gave away the asset is already paying some rent or a charge for the use of the asset, a credit will be given for this.

An important exclusion should protect elderly parents who have, for example, given a share of their home to a child, or someone else, who shares the property with them. This should assist people who give away a share of a property to someone who helps to care for them. The other circumstances in which

the new tax will not apply are:
- gifts between husbands and wives
- where property has been sold for a market price
- where the property is used only for limited visits: to babysit, for example, or for social visits
- where a full market rent is paid for using the property.

Tax experts and solicitors were, at the time of writing, still assessing the impact of the rules and were expecting all sorts of family arrangements to raise questions, including gifts between unmarried couples.

The new law is also seen by some as a clear indication that the Government has little or no sympathy for homeowners concerned about IHT bills on their properties.

The arrival of the new tax stems, in large part, from two long-running court battles between HMRC (then the Inland Revenue) and individual taxpayers over arrangements alleged by the Revenue to be in breach of IHT legislation. Two well-known cases involved a Lady Ingram and the Eversden family, and these names are often used as shorthand for a breed of creative IHT planning schemes developed by sophisticated tax planners in recent years. The details are complex, but in both cases the aim was to allow the owners of the properties involved to reduce the value of the assets to their estates but to continue to live in the properties. Other descriptions for tax planning of this type have included the double trust scheme, home loan and main residence schemes and the reversionary lease scheme.

But tax experts have been concerned that HMRC's guidance on the new system is not clear enough to show exactly under what circumstances the POAT will apply. Advisers have also warned that people who have given away assets innocently without inheritance tax in mind might be caught out and that this might not be obvious until their estates are scrutinized by the tax authorities when they die. The POAT rules apply to transactions that have taken place since 17 March 1986, which is when the rules on gifts with reservation were introduced with

IHT. The only way to escape the tax is to pay a full market rent for use of an asset or to add the value of the asset back to your estate.

People affected by the new tax had until 31 January 2007, at the latest, to decide what they would do. This was the date on which the first income tax payments were due on gifts that are caught by the POAT. The tax bill would apply to the 2005–6 tax year, which started on 6 April 2005.

Other than this, people who have given away assets from which HMRC considers they are still benefiting face income tax (POAT) charges. Such charges also apply where a donor has given someone else funds that are then used to buy an asset from which he or she benefits. A parent who gives a child cash to buy a house and then moves in with him or her within seven years may face a charge. However, if the parent moves in after seven years there will be no charge because the gift will then count as a PET. And if the parent needs care there will be no charge.

There could also be problems with gifts of part-shares in a home, depending on how much the parent is occupying compared with the share given away. Selling a share to a child and still living in the house could also make the parent liable (unless the part-sale was before 7 March 2005 and at market value). However, sales of shares in a home to commercial equity release companies are not affected.

People who had already set up IHT-saving plans that were obviously affected by the POAT had to choose whether to pay the charge or accept IHT on the value of the assets sheltered under the schemes. Those who chose to unwind the arrangements they had made faced costs to do so, including the possibility of stamp duty on the repurchase of property. In many cases, where elderly people were involved, they will have had to weigh up whether the cost of the income tax will be greater than the potential IHT bill.

If a taxpayer opted out of his or her IHT plan, and IHT became payable on death, the charge will have to be paid by the individual to whom the asset has been given. It is almost inconceivable that any of the 'packaged' schemes now caught by POAT legislation will have been entered into without advice from an accountant or solicitor – as it was mainly accountants and solicitors who devised the schemes – so hopefully those advisers will have assisted clients in untangling their arrangements.

But there remain concerns about people who could be unwittingly affected just because they made the wrong type of gift at the wrong time.

Saving inheritance tax on the family home

Some of the more creative schemes dreamed up in the past to help homeowners deal with tax on their properties while continuing to live in them were mainly the preserve of the wealthy. The new legislation has certainly limited the options for them.

It has also underlined the difficulties for anyone in this situation. And given that an estimated 2 million-plus homes face the probability of IHT bills just because of their value, many families want to know what to do about this.

There is no doubt that the problem is far-reaching.

Insurance and financial services group Prudential looked at property prices on some of London's most famous streets, immortalized in the board game Monopoly. In 2004 the average price of a house on a Monopoly street was £565,269. In theory the IHT bill on a property worth this much today would be just over £106,107 (£565,269 minus £300,000 = £265,269 at 40 per cent = £106,107) if the property were owned outright with no mortgage on it.

In 2005 the banking group HSBC conducted research looking at how much property owners would be liable to pay in IHT after taking into account the then newly introduced £275,000 threshold. HSBC calculated that the average Briton had personal assets – savings and possessions – of £55,000 each, and added this figure to property prices to get a picture of how IHT liabilities were rising or falling.

According to HM Land Registry statistics the average property price in Windsor and Maidenhead was £328,844 (December 2004). This figure, combined with the £55,000 of assets, gave a total of £383,844, £108,844 above the nil rate band at the time.

Of course, if such properties pass from one spouse to another there will be no IHT. But their children could face large bills on the death of the second parent.

The HSBC research showed that the assets of the average UK homeowner in 2005 were still £37,000 below the prevailing IHT threshold of £275,000, and that in poorer parts of the country the gap was still huge: in Hull, for example, the average homeowner, with a property worth just under £70,000, would need personal assets of £205,572 to breach the nil rate band. But HSBC calculated that the national average gap between assets and the IHT threshold had narrowed to this figure of £37,000 from £44,400 in 2004.

Nine out of ten of the UK's IHT hotspots outside London would have seen their potential inheritance tax bills rise in 2005 as a result of house price increases and despite the £12,000 increase in the IHT threshold for 2005. HSBC also estimated that the worst year-on-year increase would have been experienced by homeowners in Poole, Dorset, where the average potential IHT liability had increased by £5,102 to £11,842 in 2005.

The biggest year-on-year increase in London was in Haringey, where the average homeowner's liability rose 62 per cent to more than £22,000. Not surprisingly, Kensington and Chelsea was the nation's top hotspot for potential IHT liability. With an average property price of £717,173 the average potential bill payable in the 2005–6 tax year was nearly £199,000.

HBOS has undertaken research more recently to identify IHT hotspots around the country. It has looked at the situation in towns and in postcode areas (see tables overleaf).

Postcode districts with highest prices above IHT threshold

Postcode district	Town/City	Region	Average House Price 2006 £s	Premium to inheritance threshold £s*
SW1X	London	Greater London	1,259,050	959,050
SW7	London	Greater London	1,105,491	805,491
W8	London	Greater London	1,092,287	792,287
W1K	London	Greater London	1,063,674	763,674
SW3	London	Greater London	960,673	660,673
SW1W	London	Greater London	808,742	508,742
GU25	Virginia Water	South-East	785,215	485,215
W11	London	Greater London	751,115	451,115
SW10	London	Greater London	684,844	384,844
W1G	London	Greater London	680,324	380,324

*Average house price less IHT threshold of £300,000

Source: HBOS

Postcode districts outside South of England with highest prices above IHT threshold

Postcode district	Town/City	Region	Average House Price 2006 £s	Premium to inheritance threshold £s*
SK9	Alderley Edge	North-West	376,704	76,704
NE20	Newcastle UponTyne	North-East	376,386	76,386
B94	Solihull	West Midlands	370,213	70,213
CF71	Cowbridge	Wales	338,316	38,316
WR7	Worcester	West Midlands	322,750	22,750
CW6	Tarporley	North-West	322,095	22,095
B93	Solihull	West Midlands	316,632	16,632
B15	Birmingham	West Midlands	308,641	8,641
WR12	Broadway	West Midlands	305,360	5,360
S32	Hope Valley	East Midlands	305,061	5,061

*Average house price less IHT threshold of £300,000

Source: HBOS

Twenty towns with highest house prices above IHT threshold

Town/Borough	Region	Average House Price June 2006 £s	Premium to inheritance tax threshold £s*
Gerrards Cross	South-East	690,347	405,347
Kensington and Chelsea	Greater London	614,979	329,979
Weybridge	South-East	529,094	244,094
Westminster	Greater London	497,130	212,130
Leatherhead	South-East	481,831	196,831
Ascot	South-East	479,288	194,288
Sevenoaks	South-East	453,606	168,606
Richmond Upon Thames	Greater London	440,950	155,950
Camden	Greater London	439,835	154,835
Henley on Thames	South-East	439,048	154,048
Hammersmith and Fulham	Greater London	414,629	129,629
Hook	South-East	401,827	116,827
Godalming	South-East	388,490	103,490
Walton on Thames	South-East	379,738	94,738
Wandsworth	Greater London	364,938	79,938
Harpenden	South-East	358,816	73,816
Rickmansworth	South-East	356,764	71,764
Islington	Greater London	351,020	66,020
Dorking	South-East	350,211	65,211
Woodford Green	South-East	347,828	62,828

*Average house price less IHT threshold of £285,000 at time of price survey

Source: HBOS

Postcode districts with largest increase in the proportion of house sales above the IHT threshold over the past five years

Postcode district	Town/City	Region	Percentage of sales above £242k IHT threshold in 2001	Percentage of sales above £300k IHT threshold in 2006	Percentage point increase over 5 years
NE20	Newcastle Upon Tyne	North-East	22%	61%	40%
PL28	Padstow	South-West	10%	49%	39%
EC2Y	London	Greater London	36%	76%	39%
WR7	Worcester	West Midlands	14%	49%	35%
OX18	Burford	South-East	20%	55%	35%
TR26	St Ives (Cornwall)	South-West	4%	33%	29%
BR4	West Wickham	Greater London	27%	56%	29%
PL8	Plymouth	South-West	19%	48%	29%
IP18	Southwold	East Anglia	17%	45%	28%
NE43	Stocksfield	North	6%	34%	28%

Source: HBOS

Not only is it difficult to give away a home while you still need somewhere to live, but if you die leaving a property as your main asset your family may have to sell it to pay inheritance tax, which is normally due within six months of a death.

Case study

Susan leaves a home worth £500,000 mortgage-free to her sons. Her estate is worth £550,000 when possessions and savings are taken into account. When the nil rate band of £300,000 is deducted, the taxable amount of her estate is £250,000. At 40 per cent the bill will be £100,000, but Susan left only £30,000 in savings and since she died in June the IHT bill will be due by Christmas. If the family cannot sell the home by then they will have to look at borrowing to pay the bill or negotiate with HMRC to pay in instalments.

So, what are the main options for dealing with IHT on a family home?

- Sell up and release cash.
- Wills and trusts that leave a share in the family home to children.
- Equity release.
- Life insurance to cover the potential bill.

Selling up

A couple who bought a four-bedroom house in a leafy part of north London in the late 1950s for £2,400 put the house on the market in summer 2005 at a price of £2.4 million. One of their concerns, they told the *Daily Telegraph* newspaper, was the inheritance tax their family would have to pay on the property.

This couple had four adult children and felt that each of them needed financial help now rather than later, and the couple, who planned to move to sheltered housing, had decided to distribute the money tied up in the house to them now.

Such gifts would escape IHT if the parents survived for seven years, but otherwise the inheritance tax bill on a home worth £2.4 million could be nearly £840,000 at current tax rates (£2,400,000 minus nil rate band of £300,000 = £2,100,000 at 40 per cent).

This story is a dramatic illustration of the situation in which many elderly parents in the UK's IHT hotspot areas find themselves. Financial advisers and estate agents report that they are seeing increasing numbers of such clients deciding that the simplest way to deal with inheritance tax is to downsize.

There may also be other good reasons for downsizing, such as a desire to live in a property that is easier and cheaper to run. Some financial advisers and forecasters believe that downsizing will be a significant economic and social trend in the years to come. There could be implications for the housing market if people of middle age and upwards sell *en masse*. But estate agents – ever optimistic, perhaps – argue that the large family properties being vacated by downsizers tend to hold their value well.

Not all downsizers will want, or be able to afford, to give away the bulk of the equity they release. Some homeowners will invest the sale proceeds to provide an income. This will not necessarily solve their IHT problems – if the money simply sits in the bank it will still form part of their estate – but there are investment schemes, mainly linked to life insurance, that can be used to draw income while allowing capital to be gradually depleted or passed on free of IHT. These schemes, known as loan trusts and discounted gift schemes, are explained in more detail on pages 132 and 100 respectively. Another option is to buy an annuity with the proceeds, and there are annuity schemes tailored to deal with IHT (see also page 93).

However, there are various factors to consider before deciding to downsize, not least the emotional attachment that many people have to their homes, particularly if they have raised families there.

And it must be remembered that if the proceeds of sale are to be given away, the giver(s) must survive seven years for gifts to be completely free of IHT. There are costs associated with the sale and the purchase of a new property, and if life expectancy is poor, perhaps because of ill health, these will have to be weighed up against the potential IHT savings.

Another possibility – though perhaps remote – is that house price inflation in future will outweigh potential future IHT bills.

Using wills and trusts for IHT on the family home

Married couples might consider making arrangements to ensure that on the death of the first parent a share in the property is passed to children. The nil rate band mechanism was discussed briefly earlier in the book (see Chapter 6). Married couples have the right to pass assets to a surviving spouse free of inheritance tax – potentially a huge saving at the time of a first death. But when the second spouse dies, only one allowance (nil rate band) can be used against the value of the couple's combined estate. Tax planners have spotted ways to use the other allowance, and this form of tax planning is being used where substantial amounts are tied up in a property. But before going into more detail it is worth repeating a warning given earlier in the book (see Chapter 6) that some of these arrangements have recently come under scrutiny by HMRC, and nil rate band will trusts, the devices used to pass shares in property to children, need to be set up by solicitors knowledgeable about the latest thinking in this area. Drawn up with care, such plans should allow the surviving spouse to maintain a good deal of flexibility and control over the family home. However, this is a sophisticated area of tax planning and there can be no guarantee that the Government will not clamp down in future if it feels too much tax is being lost through such arrangements.

Plans of this kind entail getting each partner to pass on an amount up to the nil rate band of £300,000 to a trust for the benefit of the surviving family. This means that the nil rate band allowance of the first parent to die is not wasted. Potentially, the saving to the estate is £120,000.

The will provides for the nil rate band to be held in a trust for the benefit of the family, although it need not be paid straight away in cash. Trustees can, instead, ask for the surviving spouse to promise payment in future.

As mentioned earlier (see Chapter 6) there is a strong view among tax specialists, including tax barristers, that it is vital to set up these arrangements this way. The surviving spouse continues to own the property and retains the right to decide whether to sell. But the surviving spouse then has a debt to the trust that will eventually be repaid. This could be on death, but the spouse could also repay the debt later in life by, for example, moving to a cheaper home. At this point the spouse could repay some of the money owed to the trust, but he or she might still need, in effect, to borrow from the trust to fund the purchase of the new property. Later funds repaid by the surviving spouse could be used for other purposes such as to boost the finances of children or to provide school fees for grandchildren.

Solicitors have seen some nil rate band trusts with their IHT savings put into jeopardy when a family property is sold and the proceeds paid directly to the spouse when it should have gone to the trustees. Again, the importance of having the arrangements set up properly by a knowledgeable solicitor or solicitors is essential.

The more active the trust can be in regularly reviewing the needs of the family, and how they might be assisted out of the nil rate band put into the trust – albeit on loan – the better. Trustees can be the surviving spouse and other beneficiaries and/or a solicitor.

There must never be any evidence to suggest that there is any understanding that the debt will never be called in. However, the possibility of future changes in the family will have to be considered. What if the surviving spouse were to remarry? To ensure that the half of the property still owned by the spouse remains within the family, the trust would probably make the loan secured on the property, giving it rights to call on the surviving spouse's share in the same way that a secured mortgage gives a mortgage lender the right to call in a mortgage debt if a loan is not paid.

Children and the surviving spouse will be the beneficiaries of the trust. The crucial aspect of the arrangement is that the surviving partner is borrowing the share of the property formerly owned by the dead spouse. If this were not the case there would be a risk that the tax authorities would decide that the surviving spouse was having his or her cake and eating it, in other words that the whole scheme was nothing more than a gift with strings attached. In this case the share going to the surviving spouse would become liable for IHT after all.

To make this arrangement you will need to ensure that you own the property as a tenant in common (in England or Wales), rather than as a joint tenant. This gives each partner distinct ownership of a part of the property that he or she can pass on, rather than, as in a joint tenancy or joint ownership, the surviving spouse inheriting automatically.

It is also important to ensure that the trust is administered properly, which will involve annual meetings and reviews, to satisfy HMRC that this is a genuine arrangement and not an artificial one. HMRC has been looking at these schemes recently, and the setting up and maintenance of them needs to be handled carefully. You need to take advice from a solicitor who can satisfy you that he or she is confident about the mechanics of setting up such arrangements. He or she should also be comfortable talking through 'what if' scenarios concerning circumstances within the family and whether each partner in the marriage feels comfortable about giving away a share of the property.

Although tax advisers and solicitors are recommending these schemes to many clients, do not rush into one if you do not feel comfortable about the complexities. And again, be aware that there is no guarantee that HMRC will not become unhappy about such arrangements. One view is that if they become widely marketed and sold as packages, rather than being drawn up as part of personalized 'bespoke' IHT strategies, HMRC might look for ways to clamp down on them.

Equity release

An increasing number of homeowners in middle age, or older, are expected to look at equity release as a way to release capital from their properties. At the same time they may conveniently be able to reduce their potential IHT bills while continuing to live in their homes. But there are risks, and the Financial Services Authority (FSA) has expressed concern about the quality of advice being offered by people selling the schemes. It has also warned homeowners that using these schemes simply to reduce an inheritance tax bill may be short-sighted. The main concern about equity release is the extent to which interest can eat into capital, at worst possibly wiping out all of a homeowner's equity.

It is also worth noting that equity release schemes have been the subject of a major financial scandal in the past. Schemes linked to investments were sold during the 1980s but fell apart after the stock market crash of 1987, and many elderly people faced repossession as a result. The industry has been cleaned up since then, but this area is likely to be subject to enthusiastic selling by financial services companies in future, as homeowners seek ways to tap the capital in their properties and are spurred on by concern over inheritance tax. You need to be armed with the facts before rushing in. It may be simpler and cheaper to sell your home and downsize.

There are two ways to release equity without selling: take out a loan or sell a portion of your property. The main potential disadvantages to consider are the costs – including interest on borrowing, if you raise a mortgage on the property, or the loss in capital growth, if you sell a share in your home.

Equity release loans are known as lifetime mortgages. They are available in various forms. There is the 'home income' plan, to generate a regular income; interest-only mortgages, where you pay interest each month and the capital is repaid when the home is sold; roll-up loans, where interest is added to the loan for repayment on the sale of the property; and drawdown mortgages, where you withdraw smaller amounts of capital over time. A variation on the theme is the fixed-repayment lifetime mortgage, where you take out a lump sum but rather than being charged interest you agree to pay the lender more than you borrowed, when the property is sold. The amount is set at the beginning. Yet another version of the lifetime mortgage is the shared-appreciation mortgage, where you pay a mixture of interest and capital growth (from any increase in the price of the property) when the house is sold.

The other way to release equity is to sell a portion of a home outright to a specialist 'home reversion' company. You get to stay in the house but the share in the property that you have sold goes to the reversion company when the property is sold after your death. Some schemes will invest the lump sum from the sale to provide income. You do not receive the full market value for the portion of the property that you sell but usually between 35 per cent and 60 per cent less, and you do not receive any future capital growth on that portion; that goes to the company operating the scheme when the property is sold.

Normally, to take out a lifetime mortgage you will have to be in your mid-fifties at least, perhaps older. There will probably be a minimum amount that you can withdraw from your property but increasingly equity release loans are allowing homeowners to draw down funds gradually, as needed, rather than in one lump sum.

You may indeed save your family an inheritance tax bill by taking out an equity release scheme, but there are other factors to consider. The income you draw could affect means-tested state benefits and also your age-related tax allowances. You need to compare the return on any investment you make with the proceeds with interest, if you take out a loan. There will be set-up costs of several hundred pounds. But one of the most important aspects of these schemes is the cost of interest, particularly if this rolls up to be added to the original capital. At worst you could end up owing more than the property is worth, and although this would solve the inheritance tax problem it could leave your survivors with a debt to repay. Some schemes undertake to ensure that this does not happen, but you need to take into account what the arrangements would be, in this case.

A mortgage debt taken out at an interest rate of just under 7 per cent will double roughly every 10 to 11 years if all the interest is allowed to roll up. So, a loan of £45,000 at 7 per cent will work out at just under £90,000 if the property has to be sold at the end of ten years. With a home reversion scheme the loss of capital growth on the amount of your property that you sell could be more than the tax bill you were trying to wipe out.

If you want to give the proceeds of an equity release scheme to your heirs, it will be regarded as a PET – there will be no IHT if you live for seven years. Alternatively, you could put the money into a specific IHT scheme such as a loan trust or discounted gift plan (see page 132 and 100 respectively).

Case study

Consider, for instance, a property worth £1.5 million where the owner withdraws equity of £400,000 at an interest rate of more than 7 per cent. After ten years the debt has grown to more than £700,000. But if the value of the house has increased by 5 per cent a year there will still be £1,700,000 of equity in the home. After those ten years at 5 per cent, this property price inflation on the home will make it worth more than £2,400,000, but on the death of the owner the loan, now at more than £700,000, can be deducted from this along with the IHT nil rate band of £300,000 to leave a taxable amount of a little over £1,400,000. Tax at 40 per cent will be about £560,000. After deducting the debt on the property and tax on the estate, there will be £114,000 to pass on. But, had the £400,000 of equity released ten years ago been invested for survivors and had it increased at 5 per cent a year, this amount would now be worth more than £650,000. When added to the post-tax inheritance from the house, the total to pass on would be nearly £1,790,000. Without the equity release loan, tax would have been due on £2,100,000. At 40 per cent the bill would be nearly £840,000, leaving £1,560,000 to be inherited (property value of £2,400,000 minus tax at £840,000).

But be aware that house prices do not always go up and nor do investments. And if you die within seven years of giving away money raised on a property the IHT bill could be significantly larger than shown here. (Remember that PETs are counted first against the nil rate band on a death, and if they use up all of the band, and there is no taper relief available because death occurred too soon after the gift, the whole of the property value could be taxable.)

Equity release can, indeed, be an effective way to deal with inheritance tax, but should not be rushed into in panic over a possible IHT liability before you have consulted your family and obtained independent advice.

If you are looking at packaged equity release or home income plans, look for an adviser that is a member of SHIP (Safe

Home Income Plans), the trade organization operating in this industry, set up after the scandal mentioned previously in which many elderly people lost money on poorly constructed plans. SHIP operates a code of conduct related to the plans that members sell. The Financial Services Authority can supply copies of a guide to equity release via its website: www.moneymadeclear.fsa.gov.uk. Finally, it is also worth noting that while lifetime mortgages are regulated by the FSA, home reversion schemes are not.

Life insurance

For younger homeowners facing the possibility of an IHT bill on their estate, where much of the value is in a property, old-fashioned life insurance might be the simplest way to deal with the problem. It can be changed, reduced or even cancelled in future if circumstances change. After all, a property worth £500,000 now may, on paper, be capable of costing a family £80,000 in IHT, but the owners are very likely to need money from the property in future to live on. Or family circumstances might change through divorce or the need to assist children with their finances. In general, the younger you are and healthier you are when you take out life insurance the cheaper it will be. For married couples, cover will usually be arranged so that the policy pays out only on the second death, which is when the IHT bill would be payable, assuming no other arrangements had been made to deal with this. For unmarried couples who do not want to marry, policies will have to be arranged to cover bills arising after the first and second deaths as there will be no spouse's exemption. Life insurance is covered in more detail in the next chapter.

Chapter 13

Saving IHT with life insurance

Because life insurance policies can be written in trust through a simple procedure they are used as the basis for a number of inheritance tax planning schemes. Life insurance can also be combined with certain types of investments to provide an income. The basics of these schemes are outlined in the introduction to this book, but they are considered in more detail here.

Changes to the rules on trusts introduced in 2006 have affected some of the specially constructed life insurance-linked schemes used to deal with potential IHT bills. Financial advisers were still familiarizing themselves with the new regime at the time of writing and said the rules might still present questions. Most of the schemes that were available before the new rules, survived in more or less their original forms. But the amounts paid into the schemes over the nil rate band could be taxed at 20 per cent to begin with, and 6 per cent on 10-year anniversaries. Advisers say the results have been to discourage gifts of more than the nil rate band, although even if there is a charge it may be less than the potential bill for inheritance tax. Insurance-linked schemes involving the gifting of lump sums tend to be complex and vary from one product provider to another. This is an area where you will need to take advice. The crucial questions to ask are: what tax charges, if any, are payable now or in the future? And how would these charges compare with the full amount of IHT that might be payable if you had not used the scheme?

Putting pensions and simple life insurance policies into trust have been two of the simplest and most efficient ways to deal with potential IHT bills. IHT advisers say that it is still possible to put these into trust so that the proceeds can be paid without landing your estate with an IHT bill. There may be some cases where a small tax charge would apply on a tenth anniversary but life insurance policies should still be written in trust.

Basic life insurance

Basic life insurance policies are widely recommended by financial advisers to deal with potential inheritance tax liabilities. The advantages are that life insurance is relatively simple and – depending on age and health – cheap to set up, and produces a lump sum if you die that can be used to pay the inheritance tax. There are two main types of policy: term insurance, which pays out if there is a death within a certain period, and whole-of-life, which lasts for a lifetime. Insurance can be written in trust – simply by filling out a form with the life insurer – to ensure that it is paid out to a nominated survivor who can use the proceeds to pay off an IHT bill before the state has been granted probate. Otherwise, as we have seen earlier, families can come under pressure to sell a home to pay off IHT bills. A policy written in trust does not count as an asset, so there will be no tax on the amount paid out. Premiums can usually be counted as normal, routine expenditure, which means they should not constitute taxable gifts. The mechanisms are much the same as for other types of trust, but the 'magic' of life insurance is the ability to produce a large amount of money, within the trust and payable to named beneficiaries, for a relatively small outlay. As with other trusts you are giving away money earmarked for someone else, but in this case the cash materializes when you die.

As one life insurance company explains it, someone investing £3,000 a year in a life policy in trust and dying two years later might leave the trustees holding £300,000 outside the estate. To have achieved the same result by simply gifting money would have required making PETs (exempt from IHT only on survival for seven years) totalling more than £250,000, and this would have been included in the estate (potentially taxable).

So, for people who cannot afford to give away cash or property, life insurance may be the only sensible way to deal with a potential IHT liability. There is also a view that HMRC is unlikely to try to challenge this form of inheritance tax planning as it has challenged schemes that it believes contravene IHT law, in particular the gift with reservation rules. After all, insurance ensures that the IHT bill is paid, so is not a form of avoidance.

You should be looking to buy cover that will pay out a sum

Tax tip

As mentioned, one of the most useful aspects of life insurance for IHT purposes is the ability to have it written in trust so that money effectively bypasses the estate on death. It will be paid on production of a death certificate, without your estate having been granted probate, so the IHT can be settled quickly. Insurance companies will mention the option of having the policy written in trust in their documentation but often fail to explain the significance. Financial advisers say that many people do not understand that if a policy is not written in trust it will normally be counted as part of your estate when you die and could be taxed.

Tax trap

You will need to check regularly to make sure that the amount of insurance you have will cover your potential tax liability. If the value of your assets is rising, you will need to buy extra cover. If you die, the tax bill will be worked out on the value of your estate at the time of death, not on the value at the time you took out your insurance policy.

Tax trap

There can be difficulties in putting certain whole-of-life policies into trust after they have been taken out. These policies often contain an element of investment – potentially creating capital to add to your estate – and if you put one into trust some time after taking one out this may be considered a gift to the trust. In the eyes of HMRC it could be deemed a PET that could trigger a tax charge on your estate if you do not live for seven years after signing the policy into trust.

> **Tax trap**
> As we have seen earlier, taxation of gifts made within seven years of death is complex. Many people do not understand that the value of PETs made within seven years is deducted from the nil rate band at the time of death. This has the effect of eating up that allowance and possibly increasing tax on other assets left behind when you die. You can buy life insurance to cover the tax that might be payable by the recipient of a PET, but you should also consider the effect it could have on the tax on the rest of your estate. You could buy life cover to pay for this extra tax as well.

equivalent to 40 per cent of your assets over the nil rate band. The same applies to gifts that are PETs if you want to provide protection from tax for the person to whom you are giving the money or property.

The disadvantages of life insurance are that while cheap to set up the cost of premiums can be high as you get older, particularly if you have medical problems. Premiums vary from company to company but, in general, the cost of life insurance has been falling over the last few years and it may be possible to cut costs by shopping around. But at the time of writing a typical monthly premium, for a policy where the cost is fixed for life, to provide £100,000 of cover – which would comfortably cover the cost of IHT on a £500,000 estate – on the second death, for a husband aged 55 and a wife of 52, would be a little over £80 a month. A man aged 70 with a wife of 67 would pay £195. These charges assume no extra costs to reflect medical problems. It may be possible to cut the cost of cover by buying cover on what is known as a 'maximum cover' basis, where the premiums can be reviewed every ten years. The disadvantage is that premiums can rise to unaffordable levels after ten years.

Financial advisers may be able to organize a mixture of maximum cover protection and standard protection to provide an affordable plan. But the potential cost of paying for insurance over a long period of time needs to be weighed against the potential bill on your estate.

Packaged schemes with life insurance

The basis of most of these schemes is that you buy an investment-linked form of insurance, which can, of course, be written in trust. You can draw an income from the investment, but some or all of the money can pass to nominated survivors free of inheritance tax or at a reduced rate.

Gift and loan schemes

Here you lend money to a trust that invests in a single-premium life insurance bond. This provides an income for you, but the investment growth on the bond goes eventually to beneficiaries of the trust and there is no IHT to pay. The crucial aspect of this arrangement is that the money put into the trust is a loan rather than a gift and the investor draws on the loan to provide an 'income'. There could be IHT on the investment growth passed to beneficiaries of the trust.

The point of using the single-premium bond is that it can pay out 5 per cent of the capital invested (the single premium) each year and there will be no income tax to pay until the policy matures. In a gift and loan scheme these payments form the repayments for the loan you have made to the trust. You use the payments as income (the assumption is that you spend the income to live on so that you are not accumulating further assets liable to IHT). Over time, the money you put into the trust will be depleted. Normally you would make a small gift, typically £3,000 out of your annual gift allowance, to the trust at the outset and pay a larger sum in the form of the loan.

The minimum investments required by insurance companies tend to start at around £10,000.

Back-to-back schemes

Here you buy an annuity that will produce an income for life. The lump sum used to purchase the annuity reduces the size of your estate. Simultaneously you buy a whole-of-life insurance policy that aims to provide some investment growth as well as life cover. You pay annual premiums for this, funded in part by the annuity. The idea is that the life policy (written in trust) pays a lump sum, free of IHT, to beneficiaries when you die, with a fund that replaces at least some of the money lost to the estate through the purchase of the annuity. The premiums are gifts to the beneficiary, but provided the premiums can be counted as normal expenditure out of your income – without causing you hardship – they should not be caught by IHT.

You should be aware that there are varying opinions about the usefulness of these schemes. Some advisers believe that the income achieved from annuities is too low to make them worthwhile. There are also concerns that unless you set them up carefully, preferably by buying the insurance and the annuity from separate companies, HMRC will not allow the lump sum payment for the annuity to be disregarded from your estate.

These schemes are generally recommended to older investors as a way to remove capital from their estates late in life when there may be limited options for dealing with a looming IHT bill.

Discounted gift schemes

There are various types of plan on the market that can be grouped under this heading. In the past these plans tended to involve the purchase of a term insurance policy to pay a lump sum to beneficiaries after your death alongside an endowment to provide you with an income while you are alive. But more recently these schemes have involved the purchase of one or more single-premium bonds that mature in sequence to provide income. The bonds are set up within a trust and the value of the gift (to purchase the bonds) will be reduced to reflect the amount the investor might be expected to withdraw from the bond income. This reduction depends on life expectancy and the level of income the investor wants.

Case study

An insurance company gives the following example of how a discounted gift scheme would work. A woman aged 71 has an estate valued at £550,000, including some cash on deposit. She knows there could be IHT payable on her estate, but she cannot afford to give money away now as she needs it to live on. She puts £250,000 into a discounted gift scheme and asks for an income of £1,000 a month. The gift of £250,000 is 'discounted' by a little over £125,000 to reflect her expected income and life expectancy, and the value of her PET comes down to just under £125,000. The woman dies after five years and the estate is valued at nearly £425,000 (£300,000 left in the estate plus the discounted gift of just under £125,000).

Tax on the estate is worked out as follows: the discounted gift of approximately £125,000 is set against the nil rate band of £300,000. This leaves £175,000 of nil rate band unused and, when set against the remaining £300,000 of the estate, leaves £125,000 to be taxed at 40 per cent. The bill will be £50,000.

But if the woman had done nothing, the tax would have been worked out as follows: £550,000, minus the nil rate band of £300,000, to leave a taxable amount of £250,000. The tax bill at 40 per cent would have been £100,000, so there has been a saving of £50,000. Money remaining in the bond goes to her nominated survivors.

Chapter 14

Inheritance tax on homes abroad

Many Britons now own property in France, Spain and further afield. The purchase of a second home in a favourite holiday spot is such an emotional and, for most, delightful experience that the last thing on most buyers' minds will be inheritance tax. For many people the decision to buy abroad has been one made almost on impulse. That is not necessarily a bad thing, but don't labour under the delusion that homes abroad will escape HMRC's gaze when you die.

The unpalatable truth is that even if you move abroad to live, HMRC back in the UK can – depending on the overall size of your estate – levy IHT on foreign-owned property if you die. And the tax authorities in the country in which your property is located may also want a cut. You probably won't have to pay tax twice on the same asset – of which more a little later – but you need to be aware of how inheritance tax could affect second homes abroad.

From the UK point of view the crucial issue is domicile. This is a peculiarly British concept and has nothing to do with residence or even citizenship. It is about your permanent, long-term home. If you were born in Britain you will normally be considered to be domiciled here even if you live abroad for a period of time, particularly if you intend to return and make your permanent home in the UK. Domicile can affect various aspects of one's tax affairs and there is no one overarching definition of what it means. If you weren't born in Britain HMRC will normally want to charge inheritance tax if you have lived in the UK for 17 or more years out of the last 20 years.

Assuming that most UK taxpayers are domiciled there, the

point to remember is that you are liable to pay inheritance tax on all assets worldwide.

Your second home could also be affected by inheritance taxes in the country in which it is located.

- In some European countries, including France and Spain, there are laws that dictate how assets will be passed on within a family, and children take priority. It may be as important to sort out how these would affect your family as it is to deal with potential tax problems.
- Tax may be charged to individuals rather than to an estate.
- It is reasonably safe to assume that, where inheritance taxes are levied, the tax authorities in the country where your property is located will want to tax the transfer of the estate to survivors. There will almost certainly be a requirement to report the death to the authorities.
- There may be no automatic exemption from inheritance tax for spouses.
- Unmarried couples may be vulnerable to high inheritance taxes.
- You may need to make a will in the UK as well as the country in which your second property is located.
- Tax-free allowances may be significantly lower than in the UK.

The good news is that normally your family will not be expected to pay tax twice on the same asset. This is because the UK has special agreements known as double taxation agreements with several countries, and where these are not in place there may be other forms of agreement that ensure you receive a credit in the UK for tax paid abroad, or vice versa.

Another piece of good news is that in several countries, including Portugal and Cyprus, inheritance tax either does not exist or has been abolished. In Italy there is no inheritance tax but there are rules, as in France and Spain, about how assets are to be passsed on through families.

But there is no doubt that if you have property abroad and have given no thought to how inheritance tax might affect your estate, you need to do so. This is particularly so if you already know that you have a liability to inheritance tax in the UK.

It is vital to note, however, that where IHT exists in other countries the rules can be every bit as complex as in the UK. The rates of tax, allowances and legislation on how assets must be passed on can change, as they have recently in France, just as in the UK.

In Spain the amount of tax payable is determined by the relationship between the recipient of the inheritance and the deceased. Essentially, the closer the blood tie between giver and receiver, the lower the tax. There are also tax-free allowances and the calculation of an inheritance tax liability is a multi-layered project.

It may be possible to over-ride local rules about inheritance. In the past, British owners of property in Spain have often been recommended to purchase the property through a company to avoid Spanish taxes. But these arrangements have come under the gaze of authorities in both Spain and Britain and have given rise to other tax changes.

If you are considering buying a property abroad it is vital to seek local advice, or advice from a specialist in the UK, about how your foreign asset could be affected by inheritance laws in the country where your property is located, and how these could interact with UK rules.

Chapter 15

Inheritance tax if you were not born in Britain

If you were not born in the UK (which will probably mean you are not domiciled there for tax purposes) you will pay tax only on your UK assets. Domicile is not the same as residence for tax purposes, residence in the eyes of the UK immigration authorities, or even necessarily whether you hold a British passport. You might be a citizen but still have domicile abroad for tax purposes, because you were born abroad and intend to retire to that country.

However, for inheritance tax purposes the definition of domicile is clear: you will be deemed domiciled for IHT purposes if you have been resident in the UK for 17 or more of the last 20 years (and one day's residence in a tax year is enough to use up one of the 17).

For globetrotters who have lived for lengthy periods in the UK but do not necessarily expect to end their days there, there may be benefits in considering moves that would ensure they break their UK domicile, or reorganize their affairs so that they do not risk IHT on all their worldwide assets. The latter outcome would be particularly galling for people who intend to return to countries such as Canada or Australia, where IHT is not charged. You could, for example, move abroad for a period to break the UK domicile if you have acquired UK domicile by being resident for 17 of the last 20 years.

It may not be practicable or even advisable to organize your life around a potential tax bill in the UK, but a liability to UK IHT might be something you would take into consideration when making long-term plans about your life in general.

You also need to bear in mind that even if you are not domiciled in the UK your estate will still be liable to IHT on any assets held in the UK. It might be appropriate to move assets abroad to take them out of the UK IHT net, particularly if you are planning to move anyway, to your country of birth for retirement, for example.

Domicile is also relevant to married couples where one or both is non-UK-domiciled. Only £55,000 of assets can be passed on to a non-domiciled spouse free of IHT.

A UK-domiciled spouse can still make gifts during his or her lifetime to a non-domiciled spouse, which will escape IHT if the giver lives for seven years.

Chapter 16

What happens when you die

You may or may not believe in the hereafter, but there is no question that the people you leave behind to deal with your affairs will face a formidable amount of paperwork in order to account to HMRC and the probate authorities about your wealth. An understanding of the process that must take place after you die, particularly if there is likely to be an inheritance tax bill, will underline the need for anyone who owns assets of any value to keep his or her affairs in order and up to date.

If you make no arrangements to ensure there will be funds available after you die to pay an inheritance tax bill you could cause unnecessary distress to your survivors. Tax will have to be paid before probate is granted, which will cause difficulties if there is not enough cash available to do so. This burden can be particularly hard on an elderly person.

If you die leaving a will you will have appointed executors: individuals you have named who will be responsible for telling HMRC how much money you have left and for paying any inheritance tax due. If you die intestate, the people closest to you – who stand to benefit under the rules of intestacy – will be expected to act as administrators.

An estate that could be liable to inheritance tax will not be an easy one to settle. You do not necessarily have to be a solicitor to do the job but if the deceased has made a number of gifts that are taxable the calculation of tax on these may be complex.

You do not have to appoint a solicitor as an executor at the time you make your will. Your executors can appoint a solicitor to assist them if they wish, when they come to sort out your affairs. Leaving the decision to executors as to whether to appoint a professional to assist will enable them to compare fees at the time.

Your heirs will not be able to receive their inheritances until your estate has been granted probate. This will not be granted until an initial payment of any inheritance tax bill has been made, or arrangements made to pay by instalments.

Normally, your personal representatives will have to fill out a form for HMRC explaining your estate. If it is worth between £5,000 and £1 million and is not 'excepted' from inheritance tax, the personal representatives will have to fill out a full account on form IHT200.

To be 'excepted' an estate must fulfil a series of criteria, the main one being that its gross value (before deduction of debts) is less than £240,000. In this case the personal representatives fill out the four-page form IHT205.

To complete the full account on IHT200 your executors or administrators will need to do one or more of the following:

- provide a list of all assets and gifts made within seven years of your death
- search your papers to complete the account. This could include records used to file self-assessment tax returns as well as bank statements and building society passbooks
- speak to any solicitor, accountant, stockbroker or financial adviser you dealt with and also family (to make enquiries about gifts, those named in the will, business associates and banks).

HMRC will calculate the tax bill due, if requested to, but your representatives will still be required to file an account giving all the information necessary to do the calculation.

Your executors or administrators will be expected to make, in HMRC's words, 'all the enquiries they reasonably can' before submitting an account. If precise values cannot be found for assets, estimates must be produced on the basis of enquiries made (you cannot give notional figures). The fact that an estimate has been made must be clear and the exact value must be given once it is established.

An inheritance tax account must normally be filed within 12 months of the end of the month in which the death occurred. Executors can suffer penalties if they deliver accounts late or are negligent in the way an account is dealt with or delay notifying HMRC about the correct value of assets. If your executors make a mistake in the accounts they will be required to tell HMRC within six months.

After an account is submitted, HMRC will normally make additional enquiries in writing or by telephone.

Your personal representatives will also be responsible for making sure that the bill is paid. In some cases this will mean asking for money from people who received gifts from you within seven years of your death.

Since the tax must be paid before the estate is granted probate, the whole question of payment can become quite fraught, particularly if the main asset is a property that cannot be sold until probate is granted, although there are some facilities for paying by instalments.

The difficulties that can be encountered in paying IHT are one reason for ensuring that wherever possible, or practical – some policies must be used to pay off mortgages and go straight to mortgage lenders – life insurance policies should be written in trust to a survivor so that the proceeds of the policy can be paid directly to that individual. Sometimes it is necessary for executors or administrators to take out bank loans to pay IHT. Alternatively, it may be possible for them to use funds in your bank account(s), which the bank(s) will usually be able to transfer directly to HMRC. IHT bills can also be paid out of National Savings accounts and from gilts – British Government loan stock. There are also Certificates of Tax Deposit that allow for money to be put aside to pay IHT in future; interest is paid until they are drawn on by HMRC.

It is possible to pay IHT in instalments on some types of assets, including land and buildings, certain shares and timber, although interest may be charged on payments made this way. HMRC will ask for written notice that your executors want to pay by instalments, and the payments will have to be in ten equal amounts.

If an IHT bill is late, HMRC will charge interest from the due date (which must be no later than six months after your death) until the date the bill is paid. The interest will be charged regardless of the reason for the delay and whether or not HMRC has agreed the amount of tax on the due date. The rates change from time to time according to what is happening to the Bank of England base rate.

If your executors pay too much tax or interest, HMRC will pay a refund, plus interest – at the same rate that it charges on late payments – provided the overpayment is for £25 or more. If too little tax is paid, the extra amount will have to be settled later, plus interest.

Executors and administrators can appeal to Special Commissioners against HMRC decisions on the amount of IHT due. Disputes not settled at this stage may end up in the High Court or, in Scotland, the Court of Session.

It will be clear from the above that the process involved in winding up an estate where IHT is due is a big responsibility. All the more reason for anyone whose estate could give rise to an IHT bill to think clearly about who to appoint as executors. It is also vital to keep good records to help those you leave behind. The better your records, the less time and money your survivors will have to spend on sorting things out; put brutally, the less money spent on professional fees, the more there will be to pay the tax or pass on to beneficiaries of the will.

Help when there are two deaths in quick succession

It would be unfair if inheritance tax were levied twice at the full rate on the same assets within a short period of time because there were two deaths in succession. When someone dies within five years of receiving a taxed inheritance, the tax bill on their estate is reduced according to a sliding scale. The relief is applied as a percentage of the original tax bill, as outlined in the table below:

Period elapsed between deaths	Tax relief (per cent)
Less than one year	100
1–2	80
2–3	60
3–4	40
4–5	20

Chapter 17

Investing to avoid inheritance tax

If you have assets that are already causing IHT headaches it may make sense to avoid building up an even bigger IHT bill. If you are not ready to give away assets, you may want to swap some investments for others that would incur a lower IHT bill. Capital invested and growing at 6 per cent a year would double in little more than a decade, so it is worth considering options that would not give rise to further IHT liabilities.

This is likely to be true for people who are 'cash-rich' as well as 'asset-rich'. Many people now affected by inheritance tax are in the opposite position: asset-rich, because their property is the reason they have a potential liability to IHT, but cash-poor. In fact, they may even be struggling to pay bills, educate children and save for a rainy day. Where this is the case it may be necessary at this stage to simply bear in mind the fact that if or when financial circumstances are easier, and you feel you can afford to invest or save more, you should look at this alongside your liability to IHT. It will be worth considering the effect that new savings and investments will have on your IHT position. Remember that investments in ISAs, where there are substantial tax breaks on cash savings and some tax advantages for stock market investments, will not be free of IHT.

There are several types of investment that can help with IHT planning. Most, it has to be said, are more likely to suit wealthy individuals as they tend to be at the high-risk end of the investment spectrum. However, some investment management firms are now marketing products and services aimed specifically at people concerned about IHT. Most of these products are complex, although not necessarily unsuitable for investors and advisers who understand them. Swapping existing investments into others that will help you to avoid adding to your IHT liability should not be done without carefully considering the risks, not least being that if you sell investments that have made profits for you, there could be a capital gains tax bill to pay. There may be ways to deal with this, and some investments offer a double tax break: the Enterprise Investment Scheme (EIS), for example, allows an investor to defer paying CGT on gains made elsewhere when the money is put into EIS shares. There will also be costs for switching, and possibly new investment management charges. Changing a portfolio of investments should not be done without advice, but the following are some ideas to consider.

Pensions

These should be used primarily as a means to create income for retirement. But because they can be paid to survivors free of IHT through trust arrangements, they have the potential to be useful for inheritance tax savings.

Before getting carried away with this idea, though, a word of warning. Much as the Government is concerned that Britons are not saving enough for retirement, HMRC would probably become very jumpy if it thought people were putting huge amounts of money into pensions just to avoid IHT. That is not surprising given that there are big tax advantages in saving within a pension, with tax relief being given on contributions at up to 40 per cent. If people were able also to save 40 per cent of potential IHT by putting vast amounts of their assets into pensions, the Government would be unhappy. As noted earlier in the book (see Chapter 9), the Government is already moving to stop the new Alternatively Secured Pensions from being used to save IHT.

But, in general, people are not saving enough for retirement, and the IHT savings could be a useful consequence – rather than the motivating force – for making a decision that is worthwhile in its own right. Apart from the tax advantages of pension saving there can be other incentives. If you are a member of an employer's scheme the company may pay into the scheme for you, which can be seen as a form of salary top-up. So, even though pensions are a relatively inflexible form of investment, in that you cannot get your hands on the money until you retire, they should not be ignored.

At the more specialist end of IHT planning, business people and high earners are sometimes advised to use a pension scheme known as a FURB (Funded Unapproved Retirement Benefit Scheme). These do not have the same income tax benefit as conventional schemes and are aimed mainly at people who can afford to invest more than the limits on traditional pension schemes. But money invested in a FURB will not normally be counted towards the value of an estate.

Businesses

Remember the discussion of the IHT rules related to family businesses in Chapter 10? Some of the principles there – an area where there is generous IHT relief – apply to investments in certain companies. Investments in companies whose shares are quoted on the Alternative Investment Market (AIM) and (Off Exchange) OFEX – both small versions of the full stock market designed for small and growing companies – will not incur any IHT on your death provided they have been held for two years. AIM shares are increasingly being used as investments for this reason. However, it must be said that shares on the AIM are, by their nature, a relatively high-risk form of investment. These are generally smaller companies, and the tax breaks for investment exist to encourage people to help them obtain development capital. You would have to weigh the IHT savings against the risk that you could lose some or all of your money before you die.

Some stockbrokers and investment managers offer funds or pooled portfolio services where risk can be pooled and spread.

Shares in EIS companies also qualify for full IHT relief. The EIS is a Government scheme that gives a range of tax breaks on shares in companies whose shares qualify under the rules. This includes income tax at 20 per cent on the purchase of the shares and freedom from IHT once the shares have been held for two years. More information, including links to companies that specialize in advising on EIS investment, is available from the Enterprise Investment Scheme Association at www.eisa.org.uk.

Farms and woodlands

Investments in agricultural enterprises also qualify for favourable treatment under the IHT rules. The most generous relief, at 100 per cent of the value of the land, is to shield family farms from ruinous taxes.

There is increasing interest in farmland as a form of investment, partly because of the potential to save inheritance tax. But given the complexities of the rules surrounding the relief available, combined with the problems of the farming industry, this is not an investment to buy into in a hurry. It is also possible to get IHT relief on a farmhouse, which, as discussed at length already, could be an extremely valuable tax break. But HMRC will look closely at any claims for reductions in IHT bills under the rules governing farmland, and there have already been clashes between taxpayers and HMRC over this. It really is an area where specialist advice is necessary.

Investments in forests can buy you an asset that will be completely free of IHT if you live for at least two years after buying into the investment. As with other forms of investment you would need to consider the costs of the scheme and the risks before committing yourself solely to save IHT as the value of the investment can be volatile. This is also an investment that cannot usually be sold quickly if you need to get your money out, as forests acquire their value when the trees mature, which can take decades.

Lloyd's insurance market

If you invest in the Lloyd's insurance market as an underwriter – or 'name' – the value of this investment will not suffer inheritance tax. The same applies to property on which Lloyd's can call to pay debts to the market for insurance claims. However, this is a specialist and potentially high-risk investment on which you will need specific advice.

Insurance bonds

Because these can be set up so that they are held within trusts, they escape IHT. Insurance companies are constantly looking for ways to harness the tax-saving potential of trusts and life insurance to the investment products they sell. The main type of investment used in insurance-based schemes is the investment bond. These bonds are not everyone's idea of a good deal. Charges can be high and investment performance can be indifferent. For higher-rate taxpayers, however, they can be useful because income of 5 per cent of the original investment can be withdrawn each year with no immediate tax to pay, and if the bond matures when your tax rate drops – after your retirement, for example – there will be no additional tax to pay.

These can be useful if you want to draw an income from your investments.

Chapter 18

Don't try this at home: why DIY won't work with IHT

There is no getting away from it – understanding and dealing with inheritance tax is no simple matter. The more money you have, the more complicated life can become if you want to save tax for the next generation.

You might think that you can solve your family's IHT problem by simply giving money away. But have you thought about whether you can really afford to do this? And have you made a will? This is an aspect of life where it is definitely good to talk and where two heads will almost always be better than one.

Yet, despite the fact that more than 2 million households could be facing IHT bills at some time in the future because the value of their properties is more than the current tax-free IHT allowance, few people have begun to think seriously about what to do. Research by insurance company Friends Provident found that fewer than one in ten people had sought professional advice about IHT. Research by banking group Alliance & Leicester indicated that the number of people who had sought help was higher among those with assets over £275,000 (the IHT threshold at the time the research was done): one quarter had sought help. But that leaves more than three-quarters who may be unaware of the problem and what to do. In the south of England, where IHT is potentially a bigger problem than elsewhere in the UK, nine out of ten people had not sought financial advice from a qualified source.

If you have your head in the sand this could be the time to face up to the issue. Managing wealth can be costly but so can an unnecessary tax bill. You may need advice from more than one professional, for example an accountant as well as a solicitor. Or an independent financial adviser (IFA), with an all-round training in financial planning, working alongside a solicitor. This will almost certainly be the case if you want to set up a trust or trusts to help cope with a likely inheritance tax bill on your estate.

If you are wealthy enough to be giving away tens or even hundreds of thousands of pounds already, or you have a business or farm, you will almost certainly have accountants and solicitors to advise you. But people new to this area of tax will need to find suitable advisers.

What kind of advice?

Devising a strategy for dealing with inheritance tax can involve a mixture of creativity and science. Those involved in the business of advising on inheritance tax include solicitors, accountants, stockbrokers, investment managers and independent financial advisers. The knowledge required to draw up a plan and understand a client's needs could encompass pensions, investments, trusts, insurance and wills. A good adviser also needs intuition and sensitivity to family circumstances, as inheritance planning so often involves sharing money within a family.

In general a solicitor will have expertise in trusts and wills, including the ability to set up trusts and arrange for their ongoing management and administration. An accountant will know how to crunch the numbers to determine how much you are worth or what tax might be due on your gifts. But not all accountants will be able to advise competently on IHT; you need one who specializes in taxation advice for individuals. An independent financial adviser with adequate levels of training (see overleaf) should be able to take a 'holistic' approach, with a basic knowledge of what might suit but calling on solicitors or tax advisers for specialist help. An IFA is likely to know more about life insurance and life insurance-linked IHT products than a solicitor or accountant. A stockbroker may be able to offer advice on investments that save IHT; some offer specialist services in this area, as do some of the City banking firms.

If you have never sought financial advice before and are being prompted to do so because you think you have an IHT problem, use this as an opportunity to do some all-round financial planning. For example, are you saving enough for retirement and could your IHT problem be assisted by choosing particular sorts of investments? Do you have enough life insurance to ensure that a spouse or children would be able to maintain their standard of living as well as deal with an IHT bill if your wife or husband dies? Would a wedding be the cheapest way to deal with the problem if you or your partner are not married?

Finding an adviser

Before settling on an adviser, you should consider several, much as you would if you were employing someone to work for you. This may be time-consuming but, considering what is at stake, essential. Approach at least two firms. It is important to realize that the law on inheritance tax has changed recently and could change again. In addition, HMRC is vigilant about schemes it thinks amount to tax evasion rather than legitimate tax avoidance. Even where advice is in theory suitable, the execution may be wrong. One firm of London solicitors reported seeing a client who had been charged just under £300 (including VAT) by a firm of independent financial advisers to draw up a will with a nil rate band trust in it. This is a relatively low charge, but the solicitor found that there were errors in the documents that had been drawn up – family members were inadvertently omitted from the wills and documents were not witnessed properly.

Inheritance tax is an evolving area and one where, until recently, many advisers probably received few requests for assistance.

In more complex cases solicitors may consult tax barristers for opinions and this type of advice does not come cheap.

A good adviser, of course, will admit his or her inadequacies and will call in other professionals to assist where necessary.

You should also be aware that inheritance tax is a hot topic in the media, because of its relevance to increasing numbers of homeowners. Advisers will see it as an area ripe for developing new business. The best, of course, will provide sound advice for those genuinely in need of it. But it may pay to be aware that you could be open to exploitation. It is also important not to feel panicked into making arrangements that you may later regret. Don't be afraid to ask questions.

Be aware that the regulation of advisers governed by the Financial Services Authority changed in 2005. For many years there were two categories of adviser: IFAs, who were required to recommend products from across all investment companies, and tied agents, who represented just one company. Now there are three types of adviser or salesperson: those who cover the whole market, those who offer a range of products from a limited number of companies and those who represent single providers.

The new rules have also changed the way charges are disclosed to clients. The aim is to ensure that you get a clear explanation of the cost of advice so that the price quoted can be compared with that of other firms. Advisers can be paid by commission on the products they choose – which would be relevant in inheritance tax planning if insurance company bonds were used – but they must make it clear what the commission is and how the amount they are to receive compares with the market average. Importantly, firms that continue to operate as independent advisers must give clients the opportunity to pay fees rather than commission. Until recently many independents were paid mostly by commission and there has been concern that this may have affected the quality of advice.

One of the disadvantages of the new system of regulation, according to some in the investment industry, is that many good advisers will have found it too expensive to operate on a fully independent basis. There is a firmly held view that the public will not pay fees for financial advice. However, there is also a view that the new system will elevate the image of IFAs and promote only the best-informed and most highly qualified to operate in this part of the market.

It could also be argued that if people are serious about sorting out their financial affairs and making good decisions they should be prepared to pay for the services of a skilled planner.

How much?

So, how much will you pay to get advice on inheritance tax? It is impossible to be precise, particularly as you may have several aspects of your finances looked at alongside IHT planning. Putting it very bluntly, however, you won't get much independent advice for under £500. And that would just be a starting point, with extra fees to pay if you want to implement some of the more complex suggestions that might be recommended.

Fees will range up to thousands of pounds for top London legal or accountancy firms. A married couple wanting to set up wills to use both of their nil rate bands who go to see a firm of solicitors based in central London could expect to pay up to £1,000 including VAT. To set up a trust for grandchildren and make a lifetime gift to it, the cost including VAT might be around £1,200.

You may be able to negotiate a fixed fee for the service, although the solicitor may still reserve the right to charge extra if the work takes longer than originally estimated.

You also need to ask what it will cost to deal with the arrangements you make now when you die.

For a good independent financial adviser, working in conjunction with solicitors, expect to pay between £500 and £750 for an assessment including outline recommendations. If detailed recommendations are made, expect to pay between £1,000 and £1,250. The cost of implementing the recommendations could be a further £250 in addition to the solicitor's costs for wills, and, if necessary, changing the legal ownership of the property from joint tenants to tenants in common. The legal fees could come to nearly £1,000 including VAT, depending on the amount of work required.

You will need to compare the cost of advice, plus any ongoing administration and reviews, including the maintenance of trusts, with the likely saving in IHT.

For a married couple whose combined estates are worth £315,000, just £15,000 over the nil rate band of £300,000, the potential inheritance tax bill will be £6,000. If they were to set up a trust to include the value of the property up to the nil rate band on the first death, using a good firm of London solicitors, the cost of the trust arrangement after taking into account the initial fee for setting up the wills and the likely running costs of the trust after the death of the first spouse is unlikely to be enticing. But for an estate valued at £400,000, where the potential tax saving is £40,000, the same arrangement would be much more attractive. The maximum saving from nil rate band trusts – one of the few options for people with significant amounts tied up in property – is achieved for estates with a combined value of at least £600,000 (twice the nil rate band).

You will save time and money if you prepare yourself for seeing an adviser. One adviser reports that it is not unusual for couples to spend a considerable amount of time arguing over who should get what from their estates before they get down to the nitty-gritty of planning – see a relationship counsellor if this is likely to be what you do. But you can make a start on your IHT planning by using the ready reckoner on pages 124–9 of this book to work out whether you could be facing an IHT bill and, if you have not considered who should inherit, do that before sitting down in front of an adviser. A good adviser will do a detailed analysis of your estate and how it is split between the partners in a couple. But the more preparatory work you can do the better.

Start by establishing what a firm's area of expertise is. You may need to seek out an adviser with specialist qualifications.

The Society of Trust and Estate Practitioners (STEP) has members drawn from the legal, accountancy and banking professions. It runs an educational programme for professionals advising on estate and inheritance issues. To join STEP, potential members in England and Wales must have a diploma from the organization or, in the case of solicitors and accountants, submit a series of essays equivalent to the requirements of the STEP diploma.

The Chartered Institute of Taxation runs examinations for the qualification of Chartered Tax Adviser. Study is undertaken part-time over one to two years. Some advisers have just this qualification but it is common for solicitors and accountants to undertake the training after qualifying in their professions. Some independent financial advisers also take the course. Look for the letters CTA or the letters that were previously used to denote the same qualification, FTII and ATII.

The Personal Finance Society promotes high professional standards among independent advisers. Only those with advanced training gained through taking units in the Advanced Financial Planning Certificate (AFPC) are listed on its website search facility for finding an adviser. To get the minimum designation within the AFPC an adviser must pass three papers, including one on taxation and trusts that is compulsory. An adviser who has passed three papers can use the designation DipPFS. Practitioners can take up to ten units, entitling them to use the initials FPFS.

Details of the above organizations are on page 163.

Questions to ask an adviser

- How are you authorized to do business? (This might be through a professional organization or the Financial Services Authority.)
- What are your qualifications and training in relation to inheritance tax?
- Would you be calling on other professionals to assist you and would they cost extra?
- How would you be paid, by fees or commission, and how much would your service cost?
- How would this compare with my likely inheritance tax bill?
- How would your proposals affect my family?
- What if my family circumstances were to change?

- Is there a simpler option than the one you are suggesting, even if the savings are not as great?
- Could anything go wrong with the plan you are suggesting?
- Is what you are suggesting tried and tested or is there any doubt over it? (Could the tax authorities challenge it?)
- What if I could no longer afford to continue with any regular charges involved in the plan?
- Do I have to give away money to save tax and can I get it back?
- What ongoing management charges would there be, for instance for annual reviews of my affairs or for managing trusts?
- What charges would there be for my survivors in administering my affairs after my death?
- What records should I keep in relation to my inheritance tax plans?

Chapter 19

Putting it all together

Even if you have only skimmed the earlier sections of this book you will have gained some basic knowledge of how inheritance tax works and the main ways in which you can organize your finances to reduce your bill or avoid it completely.

But knowing the theory is not the same as knowing how it all works in practice. You may feel as though you are trying to find your way through a maze as you try to work out what action would be right for you. Giving money away may be one of the simplest acts in the world but, as you will know by now, there is much more to inheritance tax planning than this. Usually you need to use a variety of methods to reduce your bill, and your arrangements will need to be looked at regularly to make sure they have kept up with increases (or reductions) in the value of your assets. Some of the tools at your disposal work well at one stage of life but not at another. Some are of limited use to the very wealthy but can wipe out an IHT liability for others.

Here we begin to put the jigsaw together with at-a-glance summaries of points to consider, first by your level of wealth and then by age.

Inheritance tax planning by value of assets

Assets from £300,000 up to £2 million

- There may not be much scope to give away assets, as funds may be needed to provide income, particularly where a large chunk of money is tied up in a family home.

- Make wills to avoid paying too much IHT through dying intestate.
- Married couples should look at nil rate band will trusts to ensure that they both use their tax-free nil rate bands of £300,000 each. Splitting ownership of a family home (to become tenants in common) and leaving part to children could ultimately save the family £120,000. But wills and trusts must be carefully set up; specialist advice is needed.
- Look at life insurance to pay tax on the estate if you die. Remember to have it written in trust – probably to children, possibly to grandchildren – so that survivors have access to it immediately to pay the bill.
- Find out about insurance-based schemes, such as loan trusts (see page 132) or discounted gift schemes (see page 99) that will allow you to draw regular payments from investments. Tax tip: technically the payments are not income; usually they are regarded as repayment of capital, but there may still be money left over to pass IHT-free to survivors.
- Consider equity release (for older people) or partial sale of property (through home reversion schemes) to draw income from a family home, or to release cash to give away.
- You may not be able to afford to give money away now but remember that gifts to charity through a bequest are free of IHT.
- Consider boosting your pension savings and make sure that pensions are written in trust to avoid IHT.
- Think about marriage (if you are in a co-habiting heterosexual relationship) or a civil partnership (same-sex couple) so that assets can pass to your spouse/partner IHT-free.
- If you have a holiday home overseas, look at what the tax position would be on your death.

Assets of £2 million or more

- Consider nil rate band trusts (as above) if you are married.
- Take out life insurance (as above).
- Use insurance-linked schemes (as above), if you want to draw

regular payments from capital to supplement your income. Capital may still pass to the next generation free of IHT.

- Give money away while alive, using the £3,000 a year tax-free allowance, and others such as exemptions for gifts on marriage.
- If you want to give more than the tax-free allowances, start early with larger gifts in the hope that you will survive seven years so that there will be no tax for the estate to pay.
- Use trusts for giving; the larger the amount you give the more likely it is that you will want to exert some control over how the money is used. Be aware of tax changes from the 2006 Budget and seek advice.
- Reorganize your investments to put money into those that are immediately or potentially IHT-free such as pensions, Alternative Investment Market shares and Enterprise Investment Schemes. Seek out funds and pooled schemes to cut risk. Take care not to unwittingly trigger a capital gains tax bill.
- Consider donations to charity – if you make them while you are alive there are valuable tax breaks – or setting up your own charitable trust.
- Look at giving regularly out of surplus income (which means you must be able to maintain your normal standard of living); this could include stakeholder pensions for grandchildren.
- Marriage or civil partnership (as above).

Assets of £10 million or more

- Check the relevance of all of the above.
- Make lifetime gifts to family trusts for children and/or grand-children, but take care to avoid capital gains tax on non-cash assets.
- Where large pension funds have passed to a spouse (free of IHT) work out whether there will be IHT to pay when it passes to the next generation. Think about having it put into trust to bypass the parent's estate on death.
- Look at investment in shares that qualify for IHT relief (Alternative Investment Market shares and/or Enterprise

Investment Schemes), possibly through specially constructed pooled schemes run by investment management companies (as above).

- Consider farmland investment and/or Lloyd's insurance market.
- Gifts of heritage property may be appropriate but check the conditions: they must be accessible for the public to view.
- Specialist pension plans, such as FURBs, may be useful.

Inheritance tax planning by age

Up to 60

- Make wills, to ensure that intestacy does not lead to higher tax bills than necessary.
- Unmarried heterosexual couples should consider marriage. Same-sex couples should consider a civil partnership (as above).
- Married couples should set up nil rate band trusts in their wills (noting, as above, the need to get good advice).
- Take out life insurance to cover an IHT liability.
- Make small gifts to children, charity or others if you can spare the capital.
- Give regularly out of your income if this is possible without reducing your standard of living.
- Make the most of pension saving, as a form of investment that should be free of IHT.
- Invest in assets that do not create further IHT liabilities, such as Alternative Investment Market shares and/or Enterprise Investment Schemes.

60–70

- Make or update wills.
- Married couples and those in civil partnerships should consider setting up nil rate band will trusts.
- Assess your likely future need for income and the adequacy of

pensions to see whether giving away money will be an option in future.

- Larger gifts, including gifts to trusts, are still feasible for those who do not need the capital themselves but beware tax changes from the 2006 Budget and take expert advice.
- Consider selling the family home to release funds that can be given away.
- Think about equity release or home reversion plans on your property.
- Make larger gifts if the size of your estate, and your income, allow, remembering that the giver must survive seven years for the gifts to be completely free of tax.
- Take out life insurance, if the premiums are affordable, where other steps have not removed all IHT liability.

65–75

- Make use of wills and nil rate band planning (as above).
- Give using the annual £3,000 exemption and also the small gift allowance of £250 a year to an unlimited number of other individuals.
- Larger gifts, including gifts to trusts, are still feasible for those who do not need the capital themselves but remember that there may be tax for the estate to pay if you do not live for seven years. You may want to buy life insurance to cover potential bills in such an eventuality.
- Consider bequests through wills to charities, on which no IHT will be payable (it may be clear at this age what your income needs will be in future and whether there is surplus income and/or capital available).
- Those who want to retain income from investments could consider discounted gift schemes, where income can be drawn on money paid to insurance company investment bonds in trust.
- Take out life insurance (as above).
- Look at capital gains tax liabilities that might arise on gifts of

assets and investments (as distinct from cash). There is no CGT on death, so it may be cheaper to keep these assets than give them away now if life expectancy is not good.

75–85

- Make use of wills and nil rate band will trusts (as above).
- Gifts and smaller gifts: see above.
- Take care over larger programmes of giving, because you will not necessarily live long enough for them to be tax-free under the seven-year PET rule.
- If you have done little previous planning for IHT and want to remove money from your estate quickly, consider a back-to-back trust, where you buy an annuity and use the income from it to buy a whole-of-life insurance policy, written in trust. The annuity will stop paying out on death and the capital used to buy it is outside the estate. The income pays for the life insurance, which will pay out a sum equal to that used to buy the annuity but, being written in trust, will be outside the estate. This is a popular way to remove chunks of capital from an estate quickly and later in life.
- Make gifts to trusts.
- Life insurance may still be suitable, but this is increasingly unlikely because of the cost of premiums.
- Consider the possibility of capital gains tax (as above).

Chapter 20

Case notes

Solving an inheritance tax problem will often require the use of several different tools. Using these successfully together can take knowledge and skill. Here we look into the casebooks of a variety of financial advisers, solicitors and accountants to see what they have recommended to clients.

Creative use of trusts

Mark and Emma are married and have three children. They own a house, The Brambles, valued at £550,000, which is held jointly, and other assets (shares and savings) of £80,000, giving them a joint estate of £630,000. They are concerned about the way IHT would deplete the value of their estate for their children. The potential bill on the second death would be £132,000 (£630,000 minus £300,000 = £330,000 at 40 per cent = £132,000). But they need to make sure that if one of them dies, the other will have enough to live on. At the same time they are aware that most of their wealth is tied up in The Brambles. As things stand they will 'waste' £300,000 of tax-free allowance, because when the first dies there will be no tax to pay. They make wills that leave the value of their nil rate bands to a trust. On the first death, £300,000 of assets will pass to the trust and £120,000 of IHT will be saved. The couple need to reorganize the ownership of The Brambles so that they become tenants in common rather than joint tenants, enabling them to pass on their individual shares to someone other than each other.

In this case there is another tax-planning opportunity. Mark expects to inherit £200,000 on the death of his parents. This would mean that the couple's joint estate would be worth as much as £830,000. If Mark were to die now, instead of him giving the balance of his estate (after putting the nil rate band into trust) straight to Emma, it could go into a trust. Emma would be entitled to the income and she could also receive capital. There would be no IHT because Emma would be treated as though she had inherited the funds and, as Mark's wife, she would not pay IHT. In future the trustees could take away Emma's interest in part of the trust and transfer funds to a second nil rate band trust. Emma would be a potential beneficiary able to receive all the benefit from it. The transfer would count as a lifetime transfer by Emma – which potentially would be taxable – but if she survived for seven years there would be no tax. Please note that this second planning opportunity is no longer available as a result of new rules introduced in the 2006 Budget.

Wills and a discounted gift scheme

Joe and Claudia are a retired married couple who jointly own a house worth around £480,000. They have savings of £215,000. Their children are grown up and self-sufficient. Joe and Claudia have state pensions and some income from personal pensions and they top this up with income from their savings. They have had their wills organized so that they can pass their individual nil rate bands on to their children. They feel that they could give away £100,000 in capital if they could receive an income for life of £4,000 a year from the money, but are concerned that they could not do this and still save IHT.

Their concerns are well founded, as a gift that does not exclude the donor from benefit is treated as remaining in the donor's estate for IHT purposes. But by using a discounted gift trust from an insurance company they can put aside £100,000 for the children. The trust contains a requirement that the trustees pay £4,000 per annum to the couple each year for as long as at least one of them is alive. As with most gifts, if the couple both survive seven years the value remaining in the trust will be exempt from IHT. Even if they were both to die within seven years their tax bill would be reduced because the right to the payments of £4,000 has a value that depletes, or discounts, the value of the £100,000, which in turn reduces the amount of tax that would be payable.

The result is that £40,000 of IHT will be saved if both survive seven years. Even if both Joe and Claudia were to die within seven years, the IHT saving within seven years could be substantial.

Depending on the type of trust used, small amounts of IHT may be payable by the trust every 10 years and when it is eventually terminated after the second person dies. But if IHT rules remain similar to today's, and the nil rate band increases as it has done in the past, the £100,000 placed in trust would be unlikely to give rise to tax changes.

Loan trust

Henry is a widower aged 75 who owns a house valued at £260,000. He has savings and investments of £95,000, a state pension and a small employer's pension, supplemented by income from his investments from which he needs about £3,000 a year. His children are self-sufficient.

Henry knows that he has a potential IHT liability of £22,000, but he is reluctant to give away the £55,000 necessary to wipe out that potential liability (assuming he survives for seven years). This is because he needs the income from his savings and fears he might need the capital in the future.

Henry sets up a loan trust with an insurance company, funded in part out of his annual gift exemption of £3,000. Then he puts £50,000 into the trust as a loan, repayable on demand but where there will be regular instalments of £2,000 a year, which are repayments of capital rather than income. The £50,000 is invested in a bond. The money will still be counted as part of his estate and potentially taxable but he will spend the income and so the amount in the trust will be gradually used up, reducing his potential tax bill. He can also ask for the loan to be paid entirely if he needs capital in future. Any investment growth from the money will go to his survivors free of IHT.

Small amounts of IHT may be payable by the trust every 10 years and when it is eventually terminated but this is dependent upon the type of trust used. In this example, if IHT rules remain similar to today's rules and the nil rate band increases as it has done in the past, the £50,000 placed in the trust would be unlikely to lead to a rise in tax charges.

Using tax-free gift exemptions

Anthony, 67, is a retired businessman with a good income from pensions, savings of £250,000 and a house worth £400,000. He is single and has no children but has close friends, nieces and nephews and he would like to provide for them. He calculates that after paying his everyday bills, including tax and paying for his holidays, he has £20,000 of income to spare each year. He is happy to give this away and that once the money has been given he cannot have it back. But he does not want to hand it over straight away and wonders if he can build up a fund to pay IHT when he dies.

Anthony is advised to use this year's annual gift exemption of £3,000 and last year's unused exemption of the same amount as the initial fund for a discretionary trust. The potential beneficiaries are his family and specific named friends. The wording of the trust allows him to add other people later; he is told that being a beneficiary gives a person a right to be considered but not necessarily to receive a payment. Anthony wants to make regular payments out of his income to the trust. He needs to have proof that these payments will be regular and habitual, in order to be certain that his gifts can be free of IHT, so he writes a letter to the trustees explaining his intention to pay £20,000 a year to the trust. He encloses a cheque for that amount. Thus, the trust starts out with £26,000, but the hope is that it will grow to a reasonable size by the time Anthony dies. So long as he uses surplus income for the payments and they are on a regular basis it does not matter whether Anthony survives for seven years or not; the gifts will not count for IHT. By giving away income regularly, Anthony will build an IHT-free fund and this will also restrict the growth in his savings, further reducing his potential liability to IHT.

But what if circumstances change and Anthony cannot afford to keep up his regular payments? As long as his intentions were genuine at the time he set up the arrangements, the payments he has made so far will still be IHT-free.

Life insurance

Felix and Fiona, aged 66 and 63 respectively, are married and have two children. They have a home worth £850,000 and the mortgage is paid off. Felix has a private pension of £36,000 and the couple have savings and investments of £500,000. Their joint estate is therefore worth £1,350,000, so they are facing an IHT liability of £420,000 (£1,350,000 minus £300,000 = £1,050,000 at 40 per cent = £420,000). Felix and Fiona feel they have too many years of retirement ahead to risk giving money away, and their adult children have no pressing financial needs. But they set up nil rate band will trusts to allow both to leave part of the value of the property to trusts, so that both can use their personal IHT allowances. This will cut the bill by £120,000. Felix and Fiona are both in good health and they can well afford the premiums on a whole-of-life insurance policy that will pay out on the second death to cover the remaining tax. The policy is written in trust for the children so that it will go straight to them and will not be part of the survivor's estate.

Business relief

Andrew, 75, is a widower with two grown-up children. He has a house worth £250,000 that has no mortgage on it, and cash savings of £200,000. He receives an income of £20,000 a year from state and private pensions. Since his estate is valued at £450,000 the IHT bill would be £60,000 if he were to die now (£450,000 minus £300,000 = £150,000 at 40 per cent = £60,000). He puts money into a scheme specially designed to take advantage of IHT relief available through investment in certain qualifying businesses. It is a scheme offered by an investment management company where the underlying investment is residential property. Dividends from the company provide Andrew with an income. When the company has been trading for two years it will qualify for business relief, so the investment will be free of IHT.

Getting married

Nick and Julia have lived together for many years and have three children, one each from previous relationships and one together. They have a house in Nick's name and last year bought a run-down property as a holiday home in Julia's name, although he is paying the costs of restoring it. They have not made wills as it all seemed too complicated. But an adviser has pointed out that there would be many practical problems for their family if either were to die without a will, as the laws of intestacy would not necessarily divide their assets as they would wish: not least, the surviving partner would stand to get nothing. With their two properties the couple's survivors would also face possible problems with inheritance tax. There are also uncertainties over the properties because they are owned separately. Nick and Julia decide to get married, so as to at least postpone an inheritance tax charge if one of them were to die.

Equity release and life insurance

Zelda, 72, with two grown-up children, has an estate worth £490,000 and a potential IHT bill for her family of £76,000. Her home is worth £400,000 and she has £90,000 of investments, plus a private pension of £20,000. She takes out a whole-of-life insurance policy to pay out £140,000 on her death, and this costs £4,000 a year. The policy is written in trust to pay out to her children. She raises £80,000 by releasing 20 per cent of the equity in her property. This is invested in a property unit trust that is currently paying an income of £4,800 a year. This funds the payment of the life insurance. The equity release takes money out of Zelda's estate but the unit trust investment counts as an asset. On balance the size of her estate has not changed, but there is life insurance in place to settle the IHT bill. The amount of cover is more than the bill at its present amount, but this is to allow for increases in the future value of assets in Zelda's estate and the possibility that growth in the value of the unit trust may not be enough to make up for the compounded interest being added to the equity release loan.

Large gifts

Some years ago Kate inherited £1 million of property, a parade of shops with adjoining land, from her husband. The property had development potential, so the value of this asset could rise. Kate's financial adviser suggested that she should consider giving at least part of the value to her children and possibly their spouses and children. If Kate survived seven years the tax savings could be substantial. The property had increased in value since Kate's husband bought it, but as there is no capital gains tax on assets at death there was no need, at this point, to be concerned with CGT, although had Kate not given away part of the value at this point CGT could have become a problem in future. She gave away two thirds of the value of the property shortly before it was due to be sold for redevelopment. The children had some CGT to pay, but this was reduced by using personal CGT allowances, and, where CGT was payable, not all was at the maximum rate, because some family members were not top-rate taxpayers. Kate survived seven years from the date of the gift, making it exempt from IHT.

Downsizing

Alex and Suzie own a house worth more than the combined value of their two nil rate band IHT allowances (£600,000). One of their children is expecting a third child and wants to move to a bigger house. The other has no immediate need of funds, but is thinking about adding a conservatory to hers. The couple are advised that they could sell their own house now and move into something smaller, giving some of the balance to their children. Or they could take a mortgage out on their house to free up cash. Alex and Suzie are in their early sixties and in good health, so the chances are good that they will live for at least another seven years, in which case the gifts to the children will be exempt from IHT and they will have reduced the value of their estate.

Debt, gifts and pensions

Norman, who is married with children, is about to retire and will receive a lump sum from his occupational pension. He still has a mortgage on his property, but when the debt is repaid the full value of the house will be counted in his estate, increasing the potential IHT liability. His adviser suggests that he considers keeping the debt but giving away the pension lump sum now to his children. Norman expects that he and his wife will sell their property before long to buy something smaller, and the mortgage can be paid off at that point.

Lump sum gift to pay school fees

Gerald wants to help his son pay school fees for his grandchildren, and he has cash available to do so. He is currently paying for his elder grandson and will start paying for the younger grandson at the start of the next school year. He is advised that if he pays the whole sum now, rather than each term, he will get the whole gift out of his estate now, and by the time the children have left school the gift will be exempt because it will have been made more than seven years ago. Also, Gerald's son will be reassured that the fees would be paid even if his father were to die prematurely. Another advantage is that the school offers a discount for fees paid up front.

Regular payments for school fees

David also wants to help with a grandson's school fees but is not certain that the boy will stay the course at the chosen school. So he sets up a standing order to his son for a set sum each term. This money comes comfortably out of his income so will be wholly IHT-exempt. He is advised to fill in the specific HMRC form each year so that his executors will be easily able to claim the gifts out of income exemption.

Chapter 21

Q&A guide

Remember those questions at the beginning of the book (page 8)? Here are the answers, which provide a bite-sized summary of inheritance tax planning, together with further questions that expand on them.

1. Do married couples have to pay IHT on assets they pass on to each other?

No. So on the death of a husband or wife there is no IHT on the estate.

2. Does this also apply to unmarried couples?

No. Unmarried (heterosexual) couples cannot pass on assets free of IHT. But since December 2005, same-sex couples have this right if they register their partnerships under the Civil Partnership legislation.

3. What would the IHT bill be on an estate of £350,000 left by a widow to children?

For the 2007–8 tax year, when the IHT free allowance is £300,000, the bill would be £20,000, worked out as follows: £350,000 minus £300,000 = £50,000 at 40 per cent = £20,000.

4. Does it matter whether you make a will?

Yes. If you do not, assets will be divided according to the laws of intestacy. A surviving spouse may receive only a portion of the estate and there could be unnecessary IHT to pay.

5. If I give away money will it always be free of IHT?

Not necessarily. It depends on how much and when. There are annual allowances for lump sum gifts and separate exemptions for regular payments from income. But if you want to give away more you must survive seven years for the gift to escape tax.

6. Can I give my house to my children, continue to live in it and save IHT?

No. You cannot give away an asset and continue to benefit from it. This would be a gift with reservation. But you could give away a share of the property and invite the child to live with you and to share expenses, and then the value of the property given away would be tax-free. There can be problems under the new pre-owned assets tax (POAT) if you give cash to children to help them buy a house and then move in with them within seven years (unless this is because of ill health).

7. Do charities pay tax on legacies?

No. This is a valuable and socially useful way to deal with inheritance tax if you can afford to leave money to charities.

8. Will tax be payable on my tax-free savings: ISAs and PEPs?

Yes, PEPs and ISAs must be included in lists of assets for IHT valuations.

9. **How long will my family have to pay the tax bill after I die and can the bill be paid out of their inheritance?**

Usually the bill must be settled within six months of death, but your family may not be able to get all the money out of the estate until the bill is paid. There are facilities for getting cash from bank accounts to settle IHT early and an instalment plan where property is involved. But you need to think ahead, as paying IHT bills can be a distressing business for the bereaved.

10. **Can a will be changed after death to save IHT?**

Yes, through a deed of variation. You have two years in which to do this, and all the beneficiaries must be in agreement.

Other questions

Should I leave most of my money to my grandchildren?

If you feel that your children have enough money the answer could well be yes. Leaving money to grandchildren can be a good idea if you believe that by leaving money to your children you would simply add to their inheritance tax bill. However, this would not mean that your bequests would escape IHT. Note that giving to grandchildren while you are still alive can reduce your IHT liability by reducing the size of your estate. And you may be able to give the money tax-free by using the various relevant exemptions.

How much can I leave without paying inheritance tax?

If you are leaving everything to a spouse, there will be no IHT for him or her to pay on your death, assuming he or she is 'domiciled' for tax purposes in the UK – which broadly means that he or she was born there and that his or her permanent home is there. If money is going to other survivors you can leave £285,000 in the 2006–7 tax year and £300,000 in 2007–8.

I cannot imagine that I won't need all of my money to live on during retirement, so I don't need to worry, do I?

You need to consider what the position would be if you were to die tomorrow. If you have a potential liability to IHT your family would still have to pay a bill. You could look at life insurance to deal with this.

My husband/wife was not born in Britain. How does this affect the IHT position?

This depends on how long he or she has lived there. For inheritance tax purposes HMRC will view him or her as domiciled if he or she has lived in the UK for 17 or more of the last 20 years. If he or she is not domiciled, you can only pass on £55,000 free of IHT.

What tax will I pay on property that I own abroad when I die?

If you are domiciled in the UK – which means, very roughly, that this is your permanent home – IHT on your worldwide assets will be taxable. Your survivors may also be liable to taxes in the country where your property is located, although there are likely to be agreements between the UK and the other country to ensure tax is not paid twice.

My home is my main asset – what can I do?

Life insurance may be your best option, to cover the potential tax bill. You could set up a nil rate band will trust to put the value of the home up to the IHT nil rate band into trust for children and the surviving spouse. But this is a tricky area and needs expert advice. Older homeowners can consider selling to release cash that can be given away, or equity release.

What if I sell a share of the house to my children to raise cash?

You may be caught out by the POAT rules, so you need to get advice. You can sell to a commercial equity release company, but the rules related to family are complex and not necessarily favourable unless the parent is unwell.

Will my survivors pay tax on everything, even personal effects?

Yes, practically everything you own will be included. Tax is charged on the amount over the nil rate band, but only on the money that exceeds the band, not the entire amount. So, assets of £310,000 (£10,000 more than the nil rate band) would leave a taxable amount of £10,000, of which the bill (at 40 per cent) would be £4,000.

I've heard that there's no inheritance tax on gifts you make more than seven years before you die – but what if I die within that time?

Your gifts will be listed in chronological order and deducted from the nil rate band at the time of death. Once this tax-free slice of estate has been exhausted, your estate may have to pay tax at 40 per cent on the balance. But if you made the gift between three and seven years of death the rate will be reduced, for the recipient of the gift, on a sliding scale under a system known as 'taper relief'.

Can I save tax by setting up a trust?

Simply setting up a trust, alone, will not necessarily save you tax. The point of the trust is that it is a way of protecting assets that you have given away, and the money you put into the trust may be free of inheritance tax if it qualifies under one of the various gift exemptions. New rules were introduced in 2006 that impose immediate charges on gifts over the nil rate band into some trusts that previously did not suffer such charges. You need expert advice on trusts.

Can I give my children money to help them through university?

Yes. This counts as a gift for maintenance of the family and will be IHT-free. So no need to worry about the pre-owned assets tax rules.

How much can I give away tax-free in a year to family and friends?

As much as you like to a husband or wife as long as that person is domiciled for tax purposes in the UK. Gifts totalling £3,000 can be made to other family and friends in a tax year, plus any unused allowance from the previous tax year, and unlimited gifts of £250 each to others (but not in addition to anything given to an individual under the £3,000 exemption – you cannot give one individual £3,250 and expect the gift to be free of IHT). Parents can give up to £5,000 each to a child on marriage; grandparents up to £2,500 to grandchildren who are marrying. Gifts of up to £1,000 can be made to anyone else on marriage. Larger gifts will be free of tax if they are within the nil rate band at the time of death or you live for more than seven years after making them. Otherwise, they will be taxable, but with the bill reduced on a sliding scale depending on how long before your death they were made.

Will my heirs have to pay capital gains tax on assets that I leave them?

Not at the time of your death, but if they sell the shares, property or other assets at a profit later they may have to pay CGT. However, the profit will be worked out by comparing the sale price with the price of the assets at the date of inheritance (the base cost), not the price that you paid for the assets originally.

Something to bear in mind is that if you pass on a property there may be CGT to pay if your survivors already own homes of their own. This is because CGT is payable on properties that are not a principal private residence. But everyone has an annual tax-free allowance to cover a certain amount of profit on capital gains, so CGT will not necessarily be a problem for the people to whom you leave assets.

My husband and I own a house as joint tenants. We were thinking of switching ownership to a tenants in common basis and arranging to leave a portion of the house to our children if either of us dies, with the surviving spouse continuing to live in the house. Is it still possible to do this after the introduction of the pre-owned assets tax rules?

The new tax charge is designed for gifts made during someone's lifetime, not assets passed on at the time of death. So it is still possible to set up a nil rate band trust and leave a share of the home to children, but do take care and get expert advice; specialist legal advisers believe there is a danger that the money will not escape tax if the arrangement leaves the spouse in a position where he or she is obviously getting a benefit from something given away. Some solicitors believe the only safe way to do this is by making the value of the house in the trust a debt owed to it by the surviving spouse.

If a married couple own a property held as tenants in common, can each person leave their share of the property to a son, residing at home with his parents? It is often said that the bequeathed portion of the property goes into a trust. Is it possible to avoid the complication of a trust and for half of the property to be transferred directly to the son so the property is held by the surviving spouse and the son?

It is possible to give a share of a property to an adult son or daughter residing with the parents outright rather than putting it into a trust. Depending on the value of the property and the age and health of the parents, it might be better to make a lifetime gift of part of the property to the child. If the parent survives for seven years after making the gift this frees up the nil rate band to give more of the property to the child without paying inheritance tax. Care must be taken in the size of the share given and the proportion in which bills for property expenses are paid to avoid gift with reservation of benefit problems.

Do I need to tell HMRC about gifts I have made?

Under certain circumstances you need to. It is probably wise to check with HMRC or your advisers and it is certainly wise to keep a record of gifts so that if you die your executors will be able to show HMRC what you paid, to whom and when. Make sure that the executors of your will know where to find these records.

If you give money to discretionary trusts or to companies these may incur an immediate charge of 20 per cent – depending on whether, when added to other recent gifts, they exceed the current nil rate band. If the total value of this type of gift, in one year, is less than £10,000 and the total over ten years is less than £40,000 you do not need to declare the gifts. If your gifts fall outside these limits you will need to fill out form IHT100, obtainable from a Capital Taxes Office, and send it within 12 months, although the tax will

normally be payable before this. IHT on chargeable transfers is usually payable within six months of the gift being
made. If the gift is handed over between 6 April and 30
September the tax must be paid by the end of April in the
following year.

I have received a gift from someone. Under what circumstances should I worry about IHT?

If the person who gave you the gift dies within seven years of
making it you should tell HMRC within a year of the death.
The same is true if you have received a 'gift with reservation',
where the donor has reserved the right to use or benefit from
the gift in some way. If there is tax to pay – and there won't
necessarily be, depending on the amount and when it was
given – HMRC will expect you to pay. People who give
money that might be caught by tax can arrange life insurance
to cover the possibility that there will be a bill.

Chapter 22

Inheritance tax – the future

Inheritance tax is set to become an increasingly controversial and political topic. Where once the rising value of suburban homes was a favourite topic at social gatherings, dinner party guests are perhaps more likely now to trade ideas about how to avoid 'death tax' on the profits.

There is gathering sympathy for their plight. The banking group HBOS lobbied hard for reform before the 2005 general election and found that there were 108 electoral constituencies across the United Kingdom, mainly in the south of England, where one in every four residential property transactions was at a price above the then IHT threshold. The bank continues to publicize the impact of rising house prices on homeowners' potential liability to IHT.

The Conservative Party said in its 2005 general election manifesto that it would reform IHT if it won power. The Party argued that people whose main asset is a house are generally at a disadvantage in this area of the tax system. They are likely to pay IHT on the full value of that house, because they need it to live in, whereas families with considerable wealth in investments are likely to be able to pass on wealth more than seven years before death and avoid paying IHT on the bulk of their estates. The Government's recent pre-owned assets legislation, the Conservatives said, has made it impossible to give away a house and continue to live in it. The party also argued that it is undesirable to structure any tax in a way that encourages complex tax planning.

Ideas for reforming inheritance tax include:

- Abolition – in its 2005 general election manifesto, the

Conservative Party said that this would be the simplest option for removing some 900 pages of tax law from the statute books. But it would be a major loss of revenue. Other commentators have noted that IHT has already been abolished in some other countries, including Australia and Canada.

- Making family homes exempt from inheritance tax. An individual's main private residence is already exempt from capital gains tax when sold.
- Allowing married couples and partners to use their nil rate band twice over so that on the death of the second parent children could inherit twice the amount currently available free of IHT.
- Increasing the threshold – or nil rate band – to levels where it reflects increases in property prices, and keeping future increases in line with house prices. At the time of writing, for example, the Halifax suggested a threshold of £430,000.
- Charging a lower rate than 40 per cent.
- Charging on a sliding scale rather than at 40 per cent on everything over the nil rate band. This idea was mooted in 2004 by the Institute for Public Policy Research, a left-leaning think-tank. In a report published in August 2004 the IPPR argued that inheritance tax should be made fairer by introducing a banding system, similar to income tax, with a base rate of 22 per cent and higher bands of 40 and 50 per cent. This would mean 87 per cent of estates would pay less, but the new system would still raise an extra £147 million. The extra revenue raised from the wealthiest could be invested in assets for the poorest children through the Government's Child Trust Fund.

The future of inheritance for you

Former Prime Minister John Major once spoke enthusiastically about his vision for a nation of inheritors, where wealth would 'cascade down the generations'.

The growing concerns about inheritance tax certainly reflect a nation that is sitting on substantial assets. Yet newspapers are full of headlines about our looming retirement crisis and savings shortfall. What is going on? The short answer is that we are wealthy now but may not be able to leave much behind. Increasing longevity and inadequate pensions will force increasing numbers of baby-boomers – people nearing retirement now – to use the wealth in their homes to live on. The cost of saving for a pension entirely out of earnings is astronomical and certainly well beyond many, especially if they have to pay off loans for education before they contemplate a mortgage.

This does not mean that inheritance tax can be ignored. As we have seen, it is likely to affect millions over the next few years. HBOS has estimated that 2.3 million homes are already affected and that this could rise to 4.3 million in 2020.

Other research has estimated that one in eight people could be affected by inheritance tax in five years' time. And the reason, of course, is the mismatch between house prices and IHT allowances. Statistics from the National Audit Office show that wealth from residential housing leapt in 2004 by 12 per cent to £3,221 billion.

There are mixed signals about what the owners of this wealth plan to do with it. Research by the Alliance & Leicester in early 2005 showed that 95 per cent of Britons with estates valued at more than the then IHT allowance (nil rate band) of £275,000 wanted to pass on the house and assets to loved ones.

But research by the Joseph Rowntree Foundation at around the same time showed that passing on inheritances was a low priority among those its researchers interviewed. People liked the idea of passing on money, but two-thirds of adults with the means to make gifts said they planned to enjoy life and not worry too much.

The Rowntree research also showed a relaxed attitude towards the idea of tapping into property values through equity release. The Institute of Actuaries has estimated that homeowners may be releasing £5 billion of equity a year from their properties by 2010. Already, according to SHIP, the trade organization that represents equity release advisers, the market is 25 times larger, at £1.2 billion, than it was a decade ago.

The conclusion to be drawn from this is that we may be asset-rich now but we will die poor as we use the value of our homes to support us in old age. But this does not mean that inheritance tax can be ignored. Inheritance tax is here to stay, for middle Britain at least, until we have spent our property profits.

Owners of valuable homes and other assets need to consider how, if they themselves do not enjoy the longevity that the statistics predict, their families will deal with the bills.

The current Labour Government, re-elected for a third term in May 2005, shows no sign that it is listening seriously to cries for help from IHT-hit homeowners. The recent, larger than usual, increases in the IHT nil rate bands were dismissed by most experts as of only minimal assistance. In fact the Government, through its tax collector HMRC, shows every sign of becoming more vigilant about IHT avoidance. Last year's budget (2006) included the new tax on some of the more popular trusts used for IHT saving, as dicusssed earlier in the book, and HMRC is now looking at other trust arrangements.

Tax experts are anxiously watching HMRC's attitude to nil rate band will trusts that are being used to shelter shares in family homes from IHT. It will pay to keep a close eye on what is happening in Government policy in this area if you think you could face an inheritance tax bill in the future.

And, of course, if you already have an IHT strategy in place you should review it annually to make sure it is still effective.

Meanwhile we need to plan for the worst and hope for the best.

ABC of IHT

Glossary and terminology – some of the terms you will meet when looking into inheritance tax

Note: most of the following terms are used in the book, but some are included here because they may arise when dealing with HM Revenue & Customs or professional advisers. Others are short-hand for methods of inheritance tax planning or other aspects of this area of taxation that are described in detail in the book without using these abbreviated descriptions.

accumulation and maintenance trust
Trust often used to pass money on to children and where assets of the trust are held for the beneficiaries' maintenance, education or benefit. Money can be held to accumulate for the future, but at least one beneficiary must receive at least some of the trust's property by the age of 25. Gifts may incur an immediate tax charge as for discretionary trusts.

administrator
A person who administers the affairs of someone who has died without a will.

agricultural relief
Reduction on, or exemption from, IHT when agricultural property – land for crops or rearing of animals for food – is passed on.

agricultural value
The value of property where it can only be used solely for agricultural purposes.

annual exemption
The £3,000 you can give away each year with no IHT to pay. One of the main gift allowances for IHT purposes.

asset
A possession that has value. For calculating inheritance tax, assets will include property, personal possessions, cash and investments and anything you own jointly with someone else.

bare trust
A common and simple type of trust for holding savings for children where the money or assets are held in the name of the trustee. The beneficiary can draw income from assets held in the trust whenever they want.

beneficiary
A person who is entitled to receive property from a trust or is left money in a will.

bequest
Money, property or other items left in a will.

business relief
Relief from IHT for qualifying businesses, including family businesses.

capital gains tax (CGT)
Tax charged on profits made on an investment when it is sold. Also charged when you give something away that has increased in value while you owned it. Relatively few people pay CGT as every individual can realize a certain amount of profit in a year without being charged tax. Relevant to inheritance tax planning if you give assets away.

chargeable transfer
Gifts that do not qualify for IHT relief under the main gift exemptions, and on which there may be a 20 per cent tax charge

immediately. Usually gifts to discretionary trusts are chargeable transfers, and also gifts to companies.

chargeable value
May also be termed taxable value; value (assets minus debts) of an estate that is liable to IHT.

chattels
Personal items including clothing and jewellery, books, art, antiques and collectables, furniture and cars. Must be included when an estate is valued for IHT.

confirmation
Scotland's equivalent to obtaining grant of probate.

consideration
Payment for goods or services; can be in cash or an item of value. If the latter, the term that may be used is 'money or money's worth'.

control or controlling share
Relevant in discussions about business relief for IHT: shares that give the owner the majority of voting powers in a company.

deed of variation
Document making changes to a will after someone has died. Must be made within two years of death and can be used to change a will so that inheritance tax is saved or avoided.

Direct Payment Scheme
Inheritance tax that can be paid by transfer of funds direct from deceased person's bank account.

discretionary trust
Trust where trustees have some degree of flexibility (discretion) over who receives money. No one individual has an immediate

right to use property in the trust or receive income. Gifts to discretionary trusts may incur an immediate tax charge.

domicile
Broadly, the country considered for tax purposes to be your permanent home. Those domiciled in the UK will potentially be liable for IHT on all assets worldwide. 'Deemed domicile' is used to define whether someone has ties in the UK that are long-standing enough for IHT to be levied on worldwide estate, and is also used in relation to people not born in the UK. Deemed domicile applies, broadly, where someone has been resident for 17 or more of the last 20 years.

donor
Giver of assets.

double taxation convention or treaty
Agreement between two countries that tax will not be charged twice on the same assets.

estate
What you leave behind when you die – all assets, including property, investments, cars and other possessions. Debts and bills are deducted to work out the taxable estate.

excepted estate
Estates where a full IHT account is not required, usually because it is of low value.

executor
The person you appoint to administer your affairs after death. This includes making sure that money is distributed according to your wishes in your will.

exempt estate
Estates of £1 million or more on which there is no IHT because all passes to a spouse or charity.

exempt gifts
Gifts on which there will be no IHT payable, including: those made more than seven years before death or to husbands and wives; gifts of up to £3,000 in a tax year; wedding gifts; gifts to charities; items of national importance; small gifts of £250 per person; and regular gifts from surplus income not needed to maintain the giver's normal lifestyle.

gift in consideration of marriage
Cumbersome term to describe tax-free allowances for wedding gifts: £5,000 from a parent to a child; £2,500 to a grandchild; £1,000 to anyone else.

gift with reservation
Gift with strings attached where donor still benefits from or uses the item, in full or in part. Such gifts are not free of IHT.

GROB
GROB stands for gifts with reservation of benefit, which means that you have given something away but continue to benefit from its use. For example, giving a house away but continuing to live there. In the eyes of HMRC this is not an outright gift so it is still counted as part of your estate and will be classified as an asset when working out your IHT bill.

grossing up
Working out the gross (before-tax) amount on a sum that is paid net. Relevant to inheritance tax for calculating the value of some gifts, depending on whether tax is paid by the donor or recipient.

HMRC
HM Revenue & Customs, the department that combines the work formerly done by the Inland Revenue and Customs and Excise.

IHT
Short for inheritance tax, the tax paid on your estate (assets minus borrowings and bills) when you die.

IHT threshold
Amount at which inheritance tax starts to be charged on an estate (for amounts see nil rate band).

instalments
Arrangement by which an IHT bill on property and on some types of shares can be paid in ten annual amounts.

interest in possession/interest-in-possession trust
This is one of the main types of trust. It gives someone the right to use property or obtain an income from it immediately. Gifts may incur an immediate tax charge, as for discretionary trusts.

intestacy
Dying without having made a will. Your estate is distributed according to a pattern laid down in law. The rules vary slightly between England and Wales, Scotland and Northern Ireland. The surviving husband or wife may not be entitled to all of the deceased spouse's assets. Dying intestate can cause problems with inheritance tax.

joint tenancy
Where two or more people own property or money together and where ownership of the whole amount passes to the other(s) on the death of the first. This is a common way for married couples to own property. Relevant to inheritance tax where married couples want to split ownership of a property to pass some to survivors. See also tenants in common.

legacy
Gift passed on in a will.

life interest
Where someone has a right to benefit from an asset while alive but not to have ownership.

market value
What an asset would be worth if sold on the open market.

net
Sum equal to assets minus liability.

nil rate band
Amount of an estate that is exempt from IHT: £275,000 in 2005–6, £285,000 in 2006–7 and £300,000 in 2007–8. These figures are also known as the IHT threshold.

nil rate band will trust
Arrangement whereby someone, usually a husband or wife, writes a will passing an amount equal to the nil rate band into trust – usually for children and possibly the surviving spouse – on death. The aim is to make sure that the husband or wife can use their personal IHT tax-free allowance (there is no IHT on assets passed to a spouse, but when the second spouse dies he or she only has one allowance to set against the value of the estate).

normal expenditure out of income, or gift(s) out of income
Gifts paid out of income that is surplus to what the donor needs to maintain his or her standard of living. These are free of IHT, and can be used, for example, to fund premiums on life insurance to pay an IHT bill. The donor must be able to prove that the income was surplus to requirements.

PEP (Personal Equity Plan)
Form of tax-free investment plan no longer available to purchase new. Money still invested in PEPs counts as an asset when valuing an estate and may be liable to inheritance tax.

personal representative
Someone who carries out the administration of your affairs when you die. If there is a will the personal representative will be known as an executor, and if there is no will he or she will be an administrator.

PET (Potentially Exempt Transfer)
A gift that will suffer no inheritance tax if the giver lives for seven years after handing over the money or asset. If he or she dies within seven years there may be tax to pay if the gift exceeds the inheritance threshold (nil rate band) at that time.

POAT (pre-owned assets tax)
A new tax introduced in April 2005 to prevent people exploiting loopholes in rules about gifts with reservation. The POAT rules are complex and mean that families need to take care when parents give away assets or sell them so that they might derive benefit from them in future, for instance moving in with a child they helped with a cash gift to buy property.

quick succession relief
Special relief to make sure that where there are two deaths in quick succession, inherited money is not charged at the full rate of IHT twice.

residuary gift
Gifts from a will after all the specific gifts have been made and all debts and expenses have been paid.

reversionary interest
The right to receive assets held in trust at a certain time.

settlor
Person who makes a gift to a trust.

taper relief
Tax relief, applied on a sliding scale, that may reduce a tax bill

on a gift made within seven years of the donor's death. It is applicable if the gift exceeds the nil rate band at the time of death.

tenants in common/tenancy in common

System for holding an asset with someone else but where each share in the asset is separate from the other person's. In England and Wales, property can be owned this way or jointly. Tenancy in common is relevant to inheritance tax planning as this form of ownership – rather than joint tenancy – is necessary if a married person wants to pass a share of a property to survivors.

term insurance

Life insurance policy that will pay out a pre-determined amount of money within a certain period. Commonly used to protect mortgages in the event of a homeowner's death, and can also be used to pay inheritance tax.

transfer of value

A transfer of money that results in an individual's estate being reduced. This can be as simple as the amount of a gift, but sometimes the value of a gift reduces an estate because of the way it has been made. Two matching vases, for example, might be worth less if sold individually than if sold together. If only one is given away, the transfer of value out of the estate will be greater than half the original value of the vases as a pair.

trust

Legal entity that holds property or assets on behalf of someone else who can benefit from the assets. Various forms of trust exist, allowing varying degrees of control over who gets what, and when.

trustee

The person or persons who have legal ownership of money held in trust. They must deal with the property in the interests of the beneficiary and in accordance with the aims of the trust.

unilateral relief
Relief from IHT that may be available where someone could be taxed in two countries but where there is no double taxation agreement.

whole-of-life insurance
Life insurance that will pay out at any time during the life of the policy, widely used for inheritance tax bills.

will
Legal document setting out who should receive your assets when you die.

woodlands relief
Exclusion from inheritance tax for trees (but not land) in woodlands.

Find out more

Many of the organizations listed below have useful information on their websites about IHT and/or have links to other relevant sites.

HM Revenue & Customs
Guidance on various aspects of the rules on IHT are available from: www.hmrc.gov.uk/cto/customerguide/page1.htm
Telephone helpline: 0845 302 0900
Go to HMRC's main website (www.hmrc.gov.uk) for directions on how to obtain further information.

The Financial Services Authority (FSA)
(which regulates the financial services industry)
FSA Consumer Helpline: 0845 606 1234
Websites: www.fsa.gov.uk; www.moneymadeclear.fsa.gov.uk
The FSA does not recommend firms or give legal advice, but the Consumer Helpline can answer general queries about financial products and services. It can also tell you if a firm is authorized. Consumer Helpline hours: 8 a.m. to 6 p.m. Monday to Friday (advisers available and automated publication request service). All FSA consumer publications can be downloaded directly from the website. The FSA publishes a range of factsheets and guides, including one on equity release, *Raising money from your home* (see also the entry for Safe Home Income Plans (SHIP), below, regarding equity release).

Low Incomes Tax Reform Group

A consumer help and lobbying organization that provides information on tax and related matters aimed mainly at people on low incomes. For those over 60 on low incomes, a telephone helpline TaxHelp for Older People is provided: 0845 601 3321

There is a helpful section on inheritance tax on the website: www.litrg.org.uk

For information about giving to charity:
Charities Aid Foundation (CAF)
25 Kings Hill Avenue, Kings Hill, West Malling, Kent; ME19 4TA
Telephone: 01732 520 000
Email: enquiries@cafonline.org   Website: www.cafonline.org

To find a specialist adviser:
Accountants and specialist tax advisers:
The Chartered Institute of Taxation
12 Upper Belgrave Street, London, SW1X 8BB
Telephone: 020 7235 9381   Fax: 020 7235 2562
Website: www.tax.org.uk

The Institute of Chartered Accountants in England & Wales
Chartered Accountants' Hall, PO Box 433, London, EC2P 2BJ
Telephone: 020 7920 8100   Fax: 020 7920 0547
Website: www.icaew.co.uk

The Institute of Chartered Accountants of Scotland
CA House, 21 Haymarket Yards, Edinburgh, EH12 5BH
Telephone: 0131 347 0100
Email: enquiries@icas.org.uk   Website: www.icas.org.uk

Solicitors:
The Law Society of England and Wales
113 Chancery Lane, London, WC2A 1PL
Telephone: 020 7242 1222
Websites: www.lawsociety.org.uk; www.solicitors-online.com

The Law Society of Northern Ireland
40 Linenhall Street, Belfast, BT2 8BA
Telephone: 028 9023 1614   Fax: 028 9023 2606
Email: info@lawsoc-ni.org   Website: www.lawsoc-ni.org

The Law Society of Scotland
LP1 – Edinburgh 1, 26 Drumsheugh Gardens, Edinburgh, EH3 7YR
Telephone: 0131 226 7411   Fax: 0131 225 2934
Email: lawscot@lawscot.org.uk   Website: www.lawscot.org.uk

Association of Solicitors and Investment Managers (ASIM)
(Provides names of solicitors who specialize in investment advice)
Riverside House, River Lawn Road, Tonbridge, Kent, TN9 1EP
Telephone: 01732 783 548   Fax: 01732 362 626
Website: www.asim.org.uk

Specialists in estate planning and wills:
Society of Trust and Estate Practitioners (STEP)
26 Grosvenor Gardens, London, SW1W 0GT
Telephone: 020 7838 4890   Fax: 020 7838 4886
Website: www.step.org

The Society of Will Writers & Estate Planning Practitioners
Eagle House, Exchange Road, Lincoln, LN6 3JZ
Telephone: 01522 687 888
Email: info@willwriters.com
Website: www.thesocietyofwillwriters.co.uk

Independent Financial Advisers:
IFA Promotion Ltd
(Supplies names of up to four advisers in your area)
2nd Floor, 117 Farringdon Road, London, EC1R 3BX
Telephone: 020 7833 3131   Fax: 020 7833 3239
Website: www.unbiased.co.uk

The Institute of Financial Planning
(Register of financial advisers who operate on a fee, rather than commission, payment system)
Whitefriars Centre, Lewins Mead, Bristol, BS1 2NT
Telephone: 0117 945 2470   Fax: 0117 929 2214
Email: enquiries@financialplanning.org.uk
Website: www.financialplanning.org.uk

MyLocalAdviser
(Names of six fee-charging financial advisers within an area)
Website: www.mylocaladviser.co.uk

The Personal Finance Society
(For contact details of financial advisers with advanced training and qualifications)
20 Aldermanbury, London, EC2V 7HY
Telephone: 020 8530 0852   Fax: 020 7796 3882
Website: www.thepfs.org/findanadviser

Equity release (see also Financial Services Authority):
Safe Home Income Plans (SHIP)
PO Box 516, Preston Central, PR2 2XQ
Telephone: 0870 241 6060   Fax: 01772 840 280
Email: info@ship-ltd.org   Website: www.ship-ltd.org

Index